WALKING *with*
KATHLEEN
NORRIS

Also by Robert Waldron
published by Paulist Press

Walking with Thomas Merton
Walking with Henri Nouwen

WALKING *with* KATHLEEN NORRIS

A Contemplative Journey

Robert Waldron

Paulist Press
New York/Mahwah, NJ

Cover design by Joy Taylor
Book design by Lynn Else

Copyright © 2007 by Robert G. Waldron

All rights reserved. No part of this book may be reproduced or transmitted in any form or by any means, electronic or mechanical, including photocopying, recording, or by any information storage and retrieval system without permission in writing from the Publisher.

Library of Congress Cataloging-in-Publication Data

Waldron, Robert G.
    Walking with Kathleen Norris : a contemplative journey / Robert Waldron.
      p. cm.
    Includes bibliographical references.
    ISBN 978–0–8091–4470–9 (alk. paper)
    1. Waldron, Robert G. 2. Norris, Kathleen Thompson, 1880–1966—Appreciation. 3. Spirituality in literature. I. Title.
    PS3573.A4227Z46 2007
    813'.52—dc22

2006101514

Published by Paulist Press
997 Macarthur Boulevard
Mahwah, New Jersey 07430

www.paulistpress.com

Printed and bound in the
United States of America

Contents

≫ ≪

v

PERMISSIONS AND ACKNOWLEDGMENTS:

The Scripture quotations contained herein are from the New Revised Standard Version: Catholic Edition Copyright © 1989 and 1993, by the Division of Christian Education of the National Council of the Churches of Christ in the United States of America. Used by permission. All rights reserved.

Excerpts from *The Cloister Walk* by Kathleen Norris, copyright © 1996 by Kathleen Norris. Used by permission of Riverhead Books, an imprint of Penguin Group (USA) Inc.

Excerpts from *Amazing Grace: A Vocabulary of Faith* by Kathleen Norris, copyright © 1998 by Kathleen Norris. Used by permission of Riverhead Books, an imprint of Penguin Group (USA) Inc.

Excerpts from *The Virgin of Bennington* by Kathleen Norris, copyright © 2001 by Kathleen Norris. Used by permission of Riverhead Books, an imprint of Penguin Group (USA) Inc.

Excerpts from *Dakota: A Spiritual Geography* by Kathleen Norris, copyright © 1993 by Kathleen Norris. Reprinted by permission of Houghton Mifflin Company. All rights reserved.

"Eve of St. Agnes in the High School Gym" is from *Journey: New and Selected Poems, 1969–1999*, by Kathleen Norris, © 2001. Reprinted by permission of the University of Pittsburgh Press.

"Perennials," "A Letter to Paul Carroll, Who Said I Must Become a Catholic so That I Can Pray for Him," an excerpt from "The Monastery Orchard in Early Spring," and an excerpt from "Little Girls in Church" are from *Journey: New and Selected Poems, 1969–1999*, by Kathleen Norris, © 2001. Reprinted by permission of the University of Pittsburgh Press.

"Woman Holding a Balance, Vermeer, 1664," from *Carnival Evening: New and Selected Poems 1968–1998* copyright © 1998 by Linda Pastan. Used by permission of W. W. Norton and Company, Inc.

Dedicated with deep gratitude, respect, and affection to the memory of
M. Basil Pennington, OCSO
of St. Joseph's Abbey, Spencer, Massachusetts

Introduction

Whether or not it is an archetype embedded within the Western psyche or simply our fascination with a lifestyle that is the antithesis of contemporary life, today's readers seem unable to get enough about monasticism.

Thomas Merton's *The Seven Storey Mountain* became a national best seller in 1948 and to date has never been out of print. Nearly forty years later Kathleen Norris's *The Cloister Walk* claimed the top spot of the *New York Times* best-seller list for over a year, different from Merton's autobiography in that the person attracted to Catholic monasticism isn't a male convert but a Protestant, married woman—or to paraphrase Carl Jung—a modern woman in search of a soul.

Norris first chronicled her interest in Benedictine monasticism in her surprise best seller *Dakota: A Spiritual Geography* (1993) where she describes her unusual privilege of joining a Benedictine community for its annual retreat. This begins her love affair with the Rule of St. Benedict and *lectio divina*, both an integral part of monastic life which, she claims, have the power to sanctify people as well as time. Having abandoned religion for twenty years, Norris writes, "I rediscovered the psalms by accident, through my unexpected attraction to Benedictine liturgy, of which the psalms are the mainstay."[1]

Singing and pondering the psalms at set hours during the day transform Norris's secular perception of the world, as well as her relationship to it: she discovers order, beauty, and peace in the holy ambiance of the *Horae Cannonicae*, proving to be pathways leading to God.

Her second spiritual memoir, *The Cloister Walk*, is a journey of discovery for a writer looking for a *locus Dei*, which turns out to be St. John's Abbey in Collegeville, Minnesota, where she eventually dedicates herself as a Benedictine oblate. She writes,

> For a long time, I had no idea why I was so attracted to the Benedictines, why I kept returning to their choirs. Now I believe it's because of the hospitality I've encountered in their communal *lectio*, a hospitality so vast that it invites all present into communion with the text being read. I encounter there no God who rejects me because I can't pass some dogmatic litmus test, but one who invites me to become part of a process, the continuing revelation of holy word.[2]

She lists monastic attractions: the Benedictine motto, "*ora et labora*," the intimacy and support of communal life, monastic silence, the liturgy, the daily reading of scripture, and finally the Benedictine dictum that *everyone* is Christ. She admires how Benedictines internalize the psalms, recognizing themselves in their universality and thereby discovering their contemporary relevance. She observes, "To say or sing the psalms aloud within a community is to recover religion as an oral tradition, restoring to our mouths words that have been snatched from our tongues and relegated to the page…it counters our tendency to see individual experience as sufficient for formulating a vision of the world."[3]

The Cloister Walk records her responses to *lectio divina*, readings of the Old and the New Testament, but it's to the psalms that she is repeatedly drawn. She cites British Benedictine monk Sebastian Moore, "God behaves in the psalms in ways He is not allowed to behave in systemic theology."[4]

Abiding with monks, the acclaimed poet Norris discovers several parallels between poets and monks. To be a poet is also to embrace a singular vocation, a solitary one demanding dedication as well as prolonged periods of silence. Poets, like monks, are catalysts who cultivate openness to the possibility of epiphany because they are willing to embark upon as well as embrace the inner journey.

But writing verse, she warns, can never replace religion; she says, "the discipline of Benedict's rule has helped me to take my path toward God without falling into the trap of thinking of myself as a 'church of one.'"[5] After two extended stays at a Benedictine abbey, Norris achieves the profound insight that poetry and prayer aren't antithetical but concern both the sacred and the transcendent.

Proof of her poetic gifts is found in the book's last chapter, "Night," where there is a brief but haunting evocation of Compline (night prayer), the last of the *Horae Cannonicae*. Norris attends Compline (meaning "complete") with a friend who just learned that her sister has died. She turns to her companion, gently asking her if she would like to hear a "best bedtime story" and proceeds to recite Psalm 4, "I will lie down and sleep comes at once, for you alone, Lord, make me dwell in safety."[6] Then they both weep in shared sorrow.

Norris's third autobiographical volume, *The Virgin of Bennington*, is a frank account of her years as a student at Bennington College in the 1960s, her time as budding poet and her fortuitous finding of a mentor, Betty Kray, the driving force behind the Academy of American Poets, who successfully initiated poetry readings across America so that today it's a "given" in the life of published poets, a way for them to reach a wider audience and financially to support themselves.

When *The Virgin of Bennington* was first published, it received mixed reviews: critics and readers alike found it to be more of a memoir of Miss Kray than Norris. However, I found it illuminating for several reasons: first, Norris shares her erotic life with her readers, and this is vital biographical information if we are to understand the depth and breadth of Norris's spiritual journey in a culture blithely believing that sex is the answer to happiness. Second, Norris came into contact with some of America's finest poets: Denise Levertov, James Merrill, James Wright, Stanley Kunitz, Erica Jong, and many others. Third, she offers a summary of the state of poetry in America during the last decades of the twentieth century, and as a teacher of literature I found it to be riveting reading with inside glimpses of the lives of poets I'd read and loved, people of extraordinary gifts but at the same time ever so flawed and human.

Some have questioned Norris's judgment about being so frank about her erotic life. I remember being rather baffled after reading Thomas Merton's *The Seven Storey Mountain* in which he refers to himself as a terrible sinner, yet the only "sin" he writes about is drinking too much alcohol. Twenty years after his death we finally learned about his fathering a child while he was a student at Cambridge in England through Monica Furlong's *Merton: A Biography* (1980). Finally, I understood his deep identification with Augustine's *Confessions*, the man who prayed, "Lord, make me chaste but not now."

The sexual revolution of the 1960s made it possible for Norris to be unashamedly candid about her sexual affairs both with a woman and with men, some married. I cannot say I was shocked by her revelations, and why should I be, having read several times Augustine's *Confessions*. *The Virgin of Bennington* describes the utter loneliness Norris endured as a young woman. Later, when I read her early poetry, I noticed the predominance of the theme of loneliness, the word "alone" often appearing in her verse.

Her honesty about matters of the heart also underscores a pervading restlessness that even New York City with its excitement, bars, parties, museums, poetry readings, and even a friendship with Andy Warhol and his crowd of hangers-on could not assuage. It would take several years before Norris embraced Augustine's wisdom: "Our hearts are restless until they rest in Thee" and seek the "peace that passeth understanding" that she fortuitously stumbled upon within a Benedictine cloister. (Further comments appear in the Epilogue.)

In the tradition of Thomas Merton's *The Seven Storey Mountain*, Norris's autobiographical trilogy speaks eloquently to anyone interested in a deeper spiritual life. She herself, however, specifically identifies with twentieth-century baby boomers, a generation of

Americans "who dropped religious observance after high school or college, and are now experiencing an enormous hunger for spiritual grounding."[7] Through her life-enhancing and redemptive books, she offers us all an invitation to embark on a monastic walk, a circumambulation of the cloister of our souls.

Spring

❧ ❧

Attention Is the Moment's Annunciation

I'm now on spring vacation. Last Sunday I had an open house in celebration of my two books published in March. Twenty-five people attended. Received several beautiful spring bouquets from friends.

My former student Anthony's acrylic painting—a winter scene set up for my guests' appreciation—received much attention and praise. And for Anthony a commission!

Must soon decide on which manuscript I will concentrate this summer. My publisher expects a book on Kathleen Norris. I'd also like to finish the sequel to my novel *Blue Hope*, which has only been out a month and a half, but it's already sold over 2,200 volumes. Not bad for a book with virtually no advertising.

I think it best to work on my Norris book.

When I first saw the title of Norris's *The Cloister Walk*, I knew in an instant I'd read it; "cloister" has always been a talismanic word to me with its suggestion of the mystery and the heroism of men who totally surrender their lives to God by becoming monks.

In high school, I thrilled to Matthew Arnold's "Stanzas from the Grand Chartreuse,"

Oh, hide me in your gloom profound,
Ye solemn seats of holy pain!
Take me, cowl'd forms, and fence me round,
Till I possess my soul again;
Till free my thoughts before me roll,
Not chafed by hourly false control!

"...Fenced early in this cloistral round
Of reverie, of shade, of prayer,
How should we grow in other ground?
How can we flower in foreign air?
—Pass, banners, pass, and bugles, cease;
And leave our desert to its peace!"[8]

Unlike Arnold, I wasn't "wandering between two worlds, one dead/The other powerless to be born." I still possessed my faith, still believed that God could be experienced in this life, a divine wink gifted to those willing to embark on the mystical journey.

About a year later, I read Thomas Merton's autobiography, *The Seven Storey Mountain*, a spiritual memoir about a young man who seemingly was, indeed, offered a wink of heaven. And in my imagination, I walked with him through the cloisters of the Abbey of Gethsemani in Kentucky, chanting the psalms while kneeling on the cold stone floors of the dark church lit by beeswax candles.

Yes, cloisters were already sacred places to me, and I'd never yet been in one!

Gazing out my window, I find a pale blue morning sky. Earlier, when I put out the trash, the sky was crowded with fast-moving gray clouds—they've departed to darken another place. Good riddance!

Spring blooms everywhere. I stop my car in front of a flowering magnolia tree, the most beautiful magnolia in our neighborhood. Atop the lawn, magnolia petals are already piling up in a mauve mound. Such brief beauty: once and only once—until next year.

I open Norris's *Journey: New and Selected Poems, 1969–1999* to read "The Monastery Orchard in Early Spring." Appropriate for today:

> I, too, want to be light enough
> For this day: throw off impediments
> push like a tulip
> through a muddy smear of snow[9]

Norris yearns for lightness of being: to be awake, to be attentive, to catch the early light, to become transparent, not to allow any beauty to go unnoticed or unappreciated. But my own inner voice asks, why is it necessary to be attentive to everything? The instant answer: we have one life to live.

"I, too, want" —is Norris's demand too acquisitive? "Want" can also mean "lacking." I want because I lack.

Inattention is my lack: inattention to beauty, in particular, is my idea of a life unlived.

I drove to Cape Cod yesterday to rent a cottage for a week in mid-July. Everything I priced was much too expensive. Discouraged, I was prepared to return to Boston when I decided to visit one more place: Green Harbor in Yarmouth. Glad I did, for I found a spacious, modern condominium with a water view. A perfect location. I'm already imagining myself with a cup of coffee, enjoying the play of sunlight on the tidal flats—and reading Kathleen Norris.

I'm engrossed in Norris's *Dakota*. A stunningly beautiful memoir. Chapter one is titled "The Beautiful Places." She relishes Dakota's emptiness, its solitude, its offer of personal growth, and she is seemingly glad to be away from New York City where she had formerly resided.

Norris was born in Washington, DC, but spent most of her childhood summers in Lemmon, South Dakota. After graduation from high school, she lived in Honolulu. She later attended Bennington College in Vermont. As a young woman, she worked in New York City for the Academy of American Poets. A poet herself, she published her first volume of verse, *Falling Off*, in 1971. Other volumes followed: *How I Came to Drink My Grandmother's Piano*, *The Year of Common Things*, and *Little Girls in Church*. She no longer lives in South Dakota; after the death of her husband, David Dwyer, she returned to live in Hawaii.

Norris's love for South Dakota reminds me of when as a young urban kid, I dreamed of a life near water and woods—a solitary life like Henry David Thoreau's, one of my favorite writers. How many times I imagined diving into the crystal clear waters of Walden Pond!

Sedentary winter is over. Today I begin my walking program. Time for me to lose weight and to reduce my high blood pressure. So off I drive to the Brookline reservoir where I observe,

> A girl wearing a T-shirt and green shorts, eyes cast down and listening to her walkman.
> Two women in deep conversation, carrying individual water bottles.
> A woman tightly holding on to her cell phone.
> One dead tree.
> Dogwoods in full bloom.
> Birch trees with buds just opening, with their hanging pods.
> Japanese cherry trees in full bloom.
> Two ducks.
> Geese.
> A woman holding a fishing rod (a first!).
> Joggers.
> Blooming weeping willows, like waterfalls of pale green lace.

After a brisk twenty-minute walk, I sit on a bench dedicated to the memory of a couple who'd lived in Brookline for fifty-five years. They had likely frequented this oasis of peace bordered on one side by busy Route 9 and on the other by Tudor-style Brookline homes.

My walk is a leisurely one in a space very unlike the wide-open expanses of Norris's South Dakota. Surely not as silent, but it's quiet enough for me to be attentive to spring's first beauty. Few of the joggers and walkers take notice of what's around them, intent only on their physical regime. I say the hell with a flat stomach and rock-hard calves. I'd rather be a sponge absorbing spring's loveliness, which whispers, "Look now."

Instead of power-walking, I power-look.

Norris on Dakota's silence,

The silence of the Plains, this great un-peopled landscape of earth and sky, is much like the silence one finds in a monastery, an unfathomable silence that has the power to re-form you. And the Plains have changed me. I was a New Yorker for nearly six years and still love to visit my friends in the city. But now I am conscious of carrying a Plains silence within me into cities, and of carrying my city experiences back to the Plains so that they may be absorbed again back into silence, the fruitful silence that produces poems and essays.[10]

A visitation of heavy rains and loud, frightening thunder last night. The house shook. This morning is overcast, but the forecast promises sunshine by noon. Yesterday we shattered a weather record: it hit 93 degrees for April 17.

I carry coffee and toast into my study to listen to the birds. First opportunity for a good hearing. Unfortunately I can't name the birds residing in my yard. Doesn't matter, I'm honored to have them as guests (or am I their guest?). They're again nesting under my porch door as well as in the window where I position my summer air conditioner.

Read a few of George Herbert's poems before I pick up Norris's *Dakota*. Later, I return to Herbert after receiving an e-mail from a former student:

> Do you know Geo. Herbert's poem "The Flower"? "Who would have thought my shrivell'd heart/Could have recover'd greenness"….It is a marvel how often poetry and spiritual reading overlap, or how often one leads to the other.

Taking my student's hint, I find the poem and am delighted with it. Spring's first green is now omnipresent; it, indeed, possesses the power to re-green the soul.

Norris returns to South Dakota after a six-year stint in New York City for such a reason: to regain greenness. Dakota's silence fosters introspection; it also inspires her as a writer, its fruits being essays, poems, and eventually her book *Dakota*.

Smack in the middle of chapter two of *Dakota*, Norris quotes Thomas Merton's famous epiphany, the "Louisville Vision." (I suspected she and I were soulmates! And this year she has written the preface for the newly released *In the Dark Before Dawn: New Selected Poems of Thomas Merton.*)

That same young man who quotes Herbert (now in his early thirties and was one of my most brilliant students) sent me a stunning analysis of my novella *Blue Hope*. He concludes,

Will re-read "Blue Hope," and soon! You've given us a Vita Nuova book, reversing a famous line in the Inferno: instead of "Abandon," we have "Recover all hope, ye who enter here!" (A legend, perhaps, for the entrance of monasteries! "Ritrova la speranza!")

How gratified I am to have a former student so sensitively and intelligently respond to something I've written. In my mind's eye I still see him as a brilliant but troubled twelve-year-old boy. I'm so glad he's discovered his refuge and strength in poetry.

My handyman is hammering away downstairs. Morning quiet disperses like the birds in the tree outside my house. Today a new kitchen floor is being installed. It requires my emptying the kitchen of everything: including table, chairs, stove, and refrigerator. Fortunately I've a dental appointment this morning so I don't have to hang around. Never has a visit to the dentist looked so appealing!

Misty morning. The sun makes its grand entrance sometime around noon (says the forecast). Yesterday I admired my neighbor's flowering dogwood. Today I open Norris's *Little Girls in Church* to read,

> The dogwood tree by the poisoned Susquehanna
> is like some women in love. Breathing in soot,
> drinking water as brown
> and stinky as shoe polish,
> it gives back all it can

of blossom, and with that grace,
bows low before industrial gods of Harrisburg
men who know how things are done.[11]

How the magnolias and dogwoods on my street survive the
fumes of busses, cars, and trucks is a miracle. But every year they
come through with their beautiful blossoms, as if to say to our
modern world, "I existed before you."

Like Norris, I understand the utter importance of finding a
sacred space for soul making. I've found two places where my soul
stretches, greens, and grows: here in my study with its view of the
sky, and St. Joseph's Abbey in Spencer, Massachusetts, the setting
of *Blue Hope*. However, in my novel, I transport the abbey to
northern New Hampshire and rename it New Rievaulx.

Norris's descriptions of Dakota's wide spaces are inviting, but
would its topography appeal to my New England aesthetic, I a
devotee of Dickinson, Emerson, and Thoreau?

Norris craves asceticism because she has the sensibilities of a
monk. Monks and artists share monomania; they're driven by one
desire, the monk for God, the artist for art. However, Norris is
more complicated: she wants both God and poetry.

Derivation of monk: from the Greek word meaning "single" or
"one."

Last night's heavy rains pounded my tulips' delicate petals;
today they look like bedraggled beggars.

Weary of library copies I can't write in, I scouted the local Barnes & Noble for all the Norris books that I'd lent or given away as gifts: *The Cloister Walk* gone to Aunt Dot, *Amazing Grace* to Aunt Mary, and *Dakota* to a friend. Hardcovers, all. My new supply of paperbacks is sufficient. Anyway, I haven't any qualms about marking up paperbacks with a pen, notations I'd never allow myself in a first edition hardback.

The Norris books that I'm living with are: *Dakota*, *The Cloister Walk* (an autographed paperback, no less), *Amazing Grace, Journey: New and Selected Poems, 1969–1999, Little Girls in Church*, and *The Virgin of Bennington*.

Interesting passage in *Dakota*:

Weather Report: March 25
Suddenly, fir trees seem like tired old women stooped under winter coats. I want to be light, to cast off impediments, and push like a tulip through a muddy smear of snow. I want to take the rain to heart, let it move like possibility, the idea of change.[12]

Had I not read this description somewhere before? I open *Journey* and there it appears reworked into the poem "The Monastery Orchard in Early Spring."

The day begins with a pearl gray sky. Some blue has now worked its way through, a glimmer of hope for a nice day. My house remains in chaos. The refrigerator forlornly sits in my dining room along with the microwave and the kitchen table and chairs. Can't be put back until Monday. At least I now walk on a new kitchen floor.

A new floor, a new grounding.

New ground of being or ground of new being?

In *Dakota: A Spiritual Geography*, Norris's search for spiritual grounding ends up where it always ends: within one's soul.

Norris quotes monk Terrence Kardong, "A monk isn't supposed to need all kinds of flashy surroundings. We're supposed to have a beautiful inner landscape."[13]

I quite agree. But how does one create a beautiful inner landscape?

Or is it a matter of letting God be the landscapist?

The secret of a beautiful life, I believe, is grounded upon that to which we offer our attention. That's a scary admission when one considers to what Americans daily give their attention.

Thus, the prayer *Our Father*, "Give us our daily bread" takes on new significance. Daily bread is not problematic for many of us. But we do not live by bread alone. In fact, we have and consume too much bread. What we need is daily attention to beauty.

Plato's dictum: "We become what we behold."

New York City is an exciting place, and after 9/11, we Americans have a soft spot in our hearts for the city and its people. Having visited the Big Apple many times, I've observed its ugliness and indifference, the kind that possesses the power to destroy a

17

young budding artist. Norris was twenty-six years old when she finally left the Big Apple. For her it wasn't a sacred space (for others, it certainly could be and likely is); she didn't miss its over-stimulation or its soul-shattering noise, enjoying and eventually preferring the quieter life of the Plains.

It's now time (5:30 p.m.) for Vespers at East Coast monasteries. The birdsong outside my window must do for chant. No glorious sunset today; too many obscuring clouds have scudded in. I glimpse a silver patch of sky between the tree branches across the street, silver when I hoped to see gold.

How delighted I had been to notice Norris's *The Cloister Walk* take residence on the *New York Times* best-seller list for well over a year. It was in 1996 that Norris and Thomas Moore (of *Care of the Soul* fame) arrived on the American scene at about the same time. They're the heirs of Thomas Merton, reminding us Americans that money, cars, and fancy clothes are not the be-all and end-all of life. Like Merton, Norris and Moore exhort us to include silence and solitude in our lives. Of course, our obsession with things remains, proliferating into more sophisticated objects: computers, cell phones, VCRs, DVDs, microwaves, iPods, and so forth. As for silence: it's become as rare as clean water.

I shouldn't be smug: Can I live without my iMac and e-mail? Or my microwave oven?

When Norris became a Benedictine oblate, she promised to follow the Rule of St. Benedict. I must become more familiar with it.

My Rule? Rise early; read, write, and edit; walk around the pond; gaze upon the beauty of spring; look out my study window at the sky; and listen to the birds.

In short, my Rule is to pay attention.

In between all the aforementioned, I food shop, clean the house, wash clothes, read and correct students' essays, and cook dinner. If all is done in the spirit of Brother Lawrence of the Resurrection working in his kitchen, it's sacramental.

When Kathleen Norris and her poet husband lived in Lemmon, South Dakota, population 1,600, it was the antithesis of life in New York with its nine million people. I'll take Boston with its 550,000, a sleepy village compared to New York but a New York City when compared to Lemmon.

To find our True Self, I believe we must take locus seriously. Some people do, indeed, find sacred spaces in New York. I believe God wants me here in Boston, in my modest home with a window overlooking Church Street: here is my "cell" where I make my soul.

Geography is important, but there's always the cloister of the heart.

To more deeply understand Norris and her fascination with the Benedictines, I've purchased Esther de Waal's *A Life-Giving Way: A Commentary on the Rule of St. Benedict.* On my shelf is another of her books: *A Seven Day Journey with Thomas Merton.* She's also an expert on Celtic Christianity.

De Waal's surprising reminder: Benedict was a layman, *not* a priest and that, in its origins, monasticism was a lay movement. In chapter sixty, the Rule of St. Benedict says that priests are to be ranked "somewhere in the middle."

I rise early, before 7 a.m. Opening the *Boston Sunday Globe*, I find the interview I gave six weeks ago. Headline: "Monkish Pursuits: Teacher Heads for the Hills." In a nutshell, the caption describes my novel *Blue Hope*. The reporter Dan Smith quotes me on my students' spiritual hunger,

> The repression of the spiritual instinct is the great problem of our time. I see it in my students all the time. They have a hunger for the spiritual, and often that hunger comes out as a fascination for suicide, meaninglessness and depression.[14]

He also quotes my comment about my school being a soulless place much too deferential toward money, power, and its own reputation. When Dan recorded my comments, he asked if I minded his including them in the article. After I agreed, he said, "You're not afraid?" "No," I said, "What can they do to me?" He looked at me incredulously.

With a mug of Maxwell Lite coffee, I settle down to read the *Globe's* book section, seemingly shorter and shorter every year. Later this morning, I have to be at Trinity Church at Copley Square for a reading and book signing. Trinity is an Episcopal church, its building designed by the famous architect R. H. Richardson. As a ten-year-old kid leaving the Boston Public

Library, I noticed the beautiful church across the street. I found its door open and strode inside as if it were my parish church. I still remember its cool darkness, beauty, and mystery.

Forty-four years later, I return to sign books.

I'm well into another reading of *The Cloister Walk*. I must soak myself in Norris's books, as I had with Merton and Henri Nouwen. It might be a bit easier to do so because she hasn't written as much as they.

I vividly remember reading the *Boston Globe's* endorsement of Norris's book, "This is a strange and beautiful book. Part memoir, part meditation, it is a remarkable piece of writing....If read with humility and attention, Kathleen Norris's book becomes *lectio divina*, or holy reading."[15]

Later came the comparisons to Thomas Merton. That's all I needed to further whet my appetite.

Randomly opening de Waal's commentary on the Rule of St. Benedict I read: "During the winter season, Vigils begins with the verse: 'Lord, open my lips and my mouth shall proclaim your praise.'"[16]

My prayer is more like this: "Lord, open my eyes and I shall proclaim your beauty." Eyes that attentively see, glorify God. I have faith in sight as well as in words. However, both present potential dangers: with eyes, there may be illusion and inattention, with words, distortions and lies.

Be attentive!

One of the reasons Norris is attracted to the Rule of St. Benedict is its emphasis on communal life. Everyone gets to work in the kitchen and to take out the garbage. According to the Rule, everything also relates to God; thus, time spent in humblest activities is time sanctified.

Benedict's rule is attractive, but I'm more a person of inner rhythm, although I confess that I sometimes long for a more contemplative life centered around the structure of the holy hours: Vigils, Lauds, Prime, Terce, Sext, None, Vespers, and Compline. Their very names are alluring, suggestive of divine mystery and mystical ecstasy.

I'm used to praying when the spirit moves me or when I find the time. Another freedom is to be able to read what and when I want.

Irony: monastic structure *freed* Thomas Merton to become one of the most prolific writers of the twentieth century. I shudder to think how he would've lived without it.

Benedictine monks practice *lectio continua*, reading books in the morning and in the evening, an essential part of the flowering of contemplation. My reading of Norris is similar: I read her in the morning and later I meditate on what I've read.

Norris is enamored of the prophet Jeremiah: he's better than morning coffee! He inspires her to write verse, "Poems were coming almost every morning and, unlike my earlier work, they came out whole, and nearly finished. As I hadn't written any poetry for several years, I was extremely grateful."[17]

A powerful writer like Jeremiah opens up the unconscious because his exhortations often address repressed longings of sorrow, fear, and anger. The reader (or listener) vicariously experiences these emotions, freeing him or her to allow similar feelings to arise from the unconscious. The result is energy, sufficient to compose poems or songs or prose.

Morning begins with light, fluffy snow but by noon the sun is shining so brightly through my window that the journal page is so intensely white that I pull down the window shades in order to write. A time for everything under the sun, even shadow.

Before faith took root in Norris, she identified with poets like Louise Bogan, who said to a friend, "The gift of faith has been denied me." And Anne Sexton who told a priest, "I love faith, but have none." And John Berryman who wrote, "I would like if possible to be buried in consecrated ground."[18]

I hope Berryman, a suicide (as was Sexton), was buried in consecrated ground.

A walk around Jamaica Pond. The usually still pond is wind-whipped into wavelets, vigorously lapping the shoreline. Sights along the way: an angler wearing a red hat and sunglasses (although the sun was barely out), a duck resting on one webbed foot, and geese and black birds foraging for food, a lone white swan preening, a gray sky streaked in silver light, two elegantly svelte birches leafing and a trio of young girls sitting on a bench, laughing so hysterically that I find myself laughing—at them!

Let me not forget the scent of water mixed with the scent of flowering trees, both spiced with exhaust fumes from the cars and trucks of the Jamaica Way traffic.

The *Globe*'s interview is still being discussed in school. Students high-five me in the corridors. Several colleagues drop by my classroom, supporting my "daring but true" comments about the reality of our school.

I think of Norris courageously writing about the baby-boomer generation with their hunger to face and to tell the truth. Today their children and grandchildren must decide whether or not such a hunger is worth the necessary sacrifice. Yes, there's a spiritual famine across our land, where half-truths and outright lies have reigned—a deprivation to be faced or we'll suffer the consequences.

"Human kind cannot bear much reality," T. S. Eliot says.

Up before seven for coffee and toast. Bare tree branches etch blue shadows on the sunlit house across the street. Later at Simmons College I notice that only one of its two copper beeches has leafed, and they're only forty feet apart. The one closer east is in bloom; its leaves and branches are likely blocking the morning light so that its neighbor remains in shadow.

Norris's books attempt to bring readers closer to the light. I'm now simultaneously rereading *Dakota* and *The Cloister Walk*. I enjoy the former's "Weather Reports": they're personal and poetic, reminding me of Merton's Zen-like journal entries. In her June 30 entry she writes about her laundry day: she truly enjoys washing and hanging clothes out to dry. *Labora* (work) is as necessary in the spiritual life as *ora* (prayer), a truth St. Benedict well understood.

Norris fondly recalls her mother, a plainswoman at heart, continuing to hang out her laundry after moving to Honolulu. Norris writes,

> Hanging up wet clothes gives me time alone under the sky to think, to grieve, and gathering the clean clothes in, smelling the sunlight on them, is victory.[19]

My neighbor also hangs out her laundry. Our neighborhood is middle class, mostly people who've risen from the working class. She laments to me that her next-door neighbor complains about having to look out her window to find underwear hanging on a clothesline. She says, "What's her problem, doesn't she wear underwear?"

I smile and say nothing: epic wars erupt from such banality.

Like Brother Lawrence of the Resurrection, Norris enjoys the dailiness of life. She smells sunlight in her laundry. These days we smell fabric softeners like Bounce, advertised to smell like a "gentle breeze."

Never smells like that to me.

In class we read about Nausicca in Homer's *The Odyssey*. To prove to her parents that she's ready for marriage, she pulls a wagon of clothes to the river to wash and then arranges them on the grass to dry in the sun.

When it comes to life's basics, life hasn't changed much in three thousand years: we still wash and dry our clothes. But the world has changed for the better: men wash too!

Norris discovered Evelyn Underhill's *Mysticism*, a book that has held up well over the years, still useful in the way William James's *Varieties of Religious Experience* is still useful: both books recognize and uphold the mystical dimension of life. We now accept as classic Underhill's paradigm of the mystical journey: Awakening, Purgation, Illumination, Dark Night, and Union.

Norris considers the discipline of writing her "religion." Her sentiment is shared by poets like R. M. Rilke and Wallace Stevens. Just before his death, Stevens found true religion and was baptized a Catholic. Rilke was a cradle Catholic, only to renounce it as an adult.

Writing verse, I believe, is a spiritual exercise. The poet Charles Wright, for instance, says he writes verse as a means toward salvation, but he doesn't espouse any particular religion, although his verse is fraught with Christian allusions.

When Norris lived on the fringes of the Andy Warhol clique, she once found herself asking, "What is sin?"[20] Today it's an act of courage, especially in intellectual/academic circles, to own a smidgen of belief in the reality of sin.

She writes, "Comprehensible, sensible sin is one of the unexpected gifts I've found in the monastic tradition."[21] Her Benedictine friend says "Sin, in the New Testament, is the failure to do concrete acts of love."[22] Such a view of sin is one a twentieth-century baby boomer like Norris (and me) can live with.

After twenty years of nonattendance, Norris returns to church because "I felt I needed to."[23] To recognize and to fulfill a need requires humility. She confesses a need for both God and a nurturing communal life. Both are satisfied: she finds God through the Benedictine monks with whom she becomes friendly and through the chanting of the psalms. Of course, most of us find God through people or through books. And there's nature: Brother Lawrence of the Resurrection found God while gazing at a tree.

Books are my spiritual way.

For much of Norris's life God was a "Monster God,"[24] whom she feared rather than loved. To move from fear of God to love of God is a tremendous hurdle that only grace can overcome. And it appears to be a phenomenon that's happening everywhere throughout Christendom because we now hear more about God's *agape* (unconditional love) for us than about God's wrath, a weekly, Sunday staple of most of the homilies I heard as a youngster.

Received an e-mail today from Professor Richard Whitfield in England, along with a new poem about his dog. One verse I fell in love with: "I now long to milk the moment."

I'm milking Norris's *Dakota*, particularly the chapter titled "My Monasticism." She describes a retreat at a Benedictine monastery where silence is mandatory, even at meals. She says,

...but I had never before immersed myself in the kind of silence that sinks into your bones. I felt as if I were breathing deeply for the first time in years.[25]

Even though I live in a suburban area of well-spaced homes with wide lawns and trees, I rarely experience complete silence, or what Samuel Taylor Coleridge calls "extreme silentness."[26] The nearest to such quiet is St. Joseph's Abbey in Spencer, Massachusetts, where one can experience a silence devoid of man-made noise. Nature's "noise"—wind, rain, bird-chirping—doesn't usually disturb me. However, I find screeching brakes, car horns, neighborhood kids' screams, blaring radios, and the drone of low-flying airplanes to be annoying. I try to be detached, but if I have a choice in the matter, I prefer nature's noise.

During her Benedictine retreat, Norris writes, "Paying attention became a serious matter. 'Listen' is the first word of Benedict's Rule and of course it is silence that makes listening possible."[27]

I reach for my shelf to take down the Rule of St. Benedict. Yes, Norris is correct, the first imperative is "Listen." The next two words are "my son." Well, we can easily substitute "my daughter" for Kathleen's sake.

A perfect spring day for James Schuyler's verse. Now here is a poet who knows how to "milk the moment." His poetry stresses the transitory nature of life, espousing a "seize-the-day" lifestyle. One of his best collections is simply titled, *A Few Days*. Considering the age of the earth and the universe, we truly live for only a few days—but lifespan has little to do with the quality of living: to live well demands attention; otherwise, one merely exists.

Three birds are perched on the telephone wire; they could've easily perched on the branches of a nearby tree. Birds preferring wire to a branch, how odd! Off they fly, one at a time as setting sunlight streams through the trees' open patches; such openings disappear with further leafing, obscuring the sun until the fall when it will again be seeing-the-setting sun-through-branches time.

The Rule of St. Benedict is grounded upon the Gospels. In fact, the rule unequivocally states that the ultimate guide for our life is the New Testament.

On every news and talk show moderators discuss the sex scandal rocking the Church. The Church's shadow has flooded her consciousness. But it's not only the Church's shadow but the shadow of each of us. Carl Jung says we must embrace our shadow, forgive it, and integrate it into our lives.

Strange, that in all this discussion of scandal, I hear little about forgiveness. My heart goes out to all children abused by adults. My heart also goes out to the perpetrators. Two priests have recently committed suicide.

As horrific as these sins are, don't we Christians still believe in forgiveness—for *all* sins?

Norris writes, "Maybe it's our longing for the good in ourselves that draws us to monasteries and is realized in the reciprocal gift giving of monastic hospitality."[28] How coincidental that in class the other day I mentioned to my students that one of the great themes of Homer's *The Odyssey* is hospitality: as it applies to being either a guest and/or a host.

Father Henri Nouwen often addressed this theme, encouraging us to transform our hearts into a hospitable space for Christ. The "heart" of the Rule of St. Benedict is to render our hearts hospitable to divinity.

I'm drawn to the idea of Christ residing within my heart. Merton somewhere says that Teresa of Avila actually visualized a midget Christ abiding within her. To make our hearts hospitable to Jesus, we need only invite him into our lives. But, of course, it's always nice to hear an invitation repeated. However, Christ, I believe, visits without invitation: we too often don't know what's good for us.

During retreat, Norris listens in refectory to Sir Alec Guinness's memoir, *Blessings in Disguise*. The other day on TV, A&E devoted an hour to Guinness on *Biography*. I watched most of it, primarily to hear Guinness's elegant voice. He spoke about his acting technique which, he emphasized, is based on "less is more." The greatest acting performance, he says, is a disappearing act: the actor's personality fades away to allow the character's persona to take center stage.

Is not the spiritual dynamic similar: the ego disappears for Christ to take center stage: "It is no longer I who live, but it is Christ who lives in me"? (Gal 2:20).

Guinness admires Trappists and their "prayer without frills." While visiting a Trappist abbey, he's surprised, however, to find the monks a bit garrulous. My experience has been the opposite: St. Joseph's Abbey's monks tend not to engage visitors in small talk. As a guest, I abide by their rules, reluctant to engage them in conversation. A mutual smile suffices. Anyway, what would I say to people I consider living icons?

Norris mentions her hairdresser's visit to St. Joseph's Abbey. His life was never the same: "They blew me away," adding an expletive I can't include here. A similar, life-transforming experience happened to me in the early 1970s when I first met Father Thomas Keating. We didn't say much to each other, but I knew I was in the presence of holiness, and never forgot it. At the recent funeral for Father Basil Pennington, I met him again, and my initial response was reinforced.

Without a doubt, Norris's *Dakota* is one of the most remarkable spiritual autobiographies to be written in the twentieth century. Along with lyrically descriptive images of the wide-open spaces of the South Dakota landscape, she reveals with a glad heart her newly discovered blooming soulscape. She's gradually become a person who allows people into her now hospitable heart. By God's grace, she found the hospitable heart of the Benedictines, who help her to open her heart to people and to God.

Norris quotes Father Matthew Kelty several times. I first came across Father Kelty in his autobiographical *Flute Solo*, a lovely memoir of his time spent as a hermit in New Guinea. His interest in Carl Jung fueled my own interest in the Swiss psychiatrist whom I'd just discovered.

Later, I had the good fortune to travel to Gethsemani to meet Father Kelty (as well as Brother Patrick Hart, also a man of tremendous generosity). Father Kelty is the personification of friendliness and humility: in Jungian terms he is an integrated man (now an elderly monk, still residing at Gethsemani). He spoke lovingly of Thomas Merton, under whom he studied as a novice and later had the privilege of typing Merton's manuscripts.

Father Kelty believes that a man not in touch with his *anima* wouldn't make a good contemplative monk. And judging by Norris's close, enriching friendship with Benedictine men, I'd have to say she's in touch with her *animus*.

I understand Norris's attraction to monasteries. They serve as reminders to us that people can peacefully live together, that possessions can indeed be shared, that no one is greater than another. An abbey is a Utopian society on a microcosmic level. But like Thomas Merton, I don't believe it can exist on the macrocosmic level: people are by nature far too competitive and acquisitive, their egos too often demanding attention, aggrandizement, and rewards.

While reading *Dakota*, I notice Norris's intense capacity to see. Nothing escapes her eye: deer bounding across a field, cloudbursts, trees and their shade, blooming flowers, sudden rain and mist—and they all still astonish her.

I also have an impression of her often looking up at the ever-changing sky. She couldn't do it in New York with its towering skyscrapers, edifices that not so much scrape the sky as obscure it!

When a book is as engrossing as *Dakota* is, I'm sad to come to its last page. Such a feeling usually means I'll likely reread it in the future.

I'm now focusing on *The Cloister Walk*. I'm at the section where she writes eloquently about the psalms, inspiring me to read a few before I turn in tonight.

Norris writes, "the psalms act as good psychologists."[29] I understand what she means; in past readings of psalms I've met my shadow: my anger, my jealousy, my cursing, and my smallness.

Norris writes, "The psalms are full of shadows—enemies, stark images of betrayal…."[30] To read the psalms is to read our own spiritual journey.

About the Psalter, Norris says,

But its true theme is a desire for the holy that, whatever form it takes, seems to be a part of the human condition, a desire easily forgotten in the pull and tug of daily life, where groans of despair can predominate.[31]

New Resolve: daily to read the psalms. It's a good way to join my prayer with the prayer of monastic communities all around the world. It almost goes without saying that it's a good way for anyone to get in touch with his or her shadow, those repressed parts of ourselves we keep from the light of consciousness: the guilt, the failures, even our lost ideals now smoldering in darkness, lodged with our life's repressed disappointments and hurts.

Dull, gray, cold day. Winter can't seem to release its clutch of spring's skirts. At night, I switch the heat on. The forecast promises a warm weekend. Glad to hear it, for I have a busy schedule: Saturday a reading of *Blue Hope* at Borders in Braintree at 2 p.m.; Sunday the Merton Chapter's bimonthly meeting.

I'm considering a Kathleen Norris Retreat at St. Stephen Priory this coming fall. I should call Pam, the priory's secretary, to check for a free October weekend. Fall bookings are popular at the priory, an astonishingly beautiful place in autumn (the Dominicans have recently sold it to Boston College).

Bede Griffith's comment about the psalms: they are songs of the old order to be replaced by Jesus' command to love thy neighbor as thyself, the Jesus who says to forgive 70 x 7 times, the Jesus who says to turn the other cheek.

The Copper Beech tree at Simmons College hasn't died. Today I notice bursting buds, a magnificent tree, stately like no other tree.

On my street not too long ago an ancient tree had to be cut down. The people who "owned" it held a wake. As it was carted away in chopped pieces (likely to be used as firewood), they raised their glasses of wine in farewell. Some might snicker, but I was moved by their emotional farewell.

Monks and women: Norris finds that today's monks are far from hostile to women. They feel comfortable around women because they're in touch with their *anima*, having won an inner marriage of opposites.

Norris frankly credits a homosexual Benedictine monk as her wisest confidant. Surely with a husband who suffers from depression, Norris is often called upon to be the nurturer. Her turning to a homosexual monk for counsel isn't surprising: he could be considered marginal both as a monk *and* as a man. Perhaps he understands more deeply than most the frightening and lonely abysses many people stare or fall into.

Thomas Merton profoundly understood marginality, observing that as a solitary monk, he faced and explored issues in his life that most people couldn't examine unless they were in therapy.

Norris is an earthy mystic, expressing her opinions in rather colorful language, language I couldn't use in my classroom.

Norris is an effective and creative teacher of verse; she encourages youngsters to write poems, winning success in drawing out even the most reluctant students. She profoundly understands that poetry is the language of the soul, both for adults and children.

Being a parent isn't the *sine qua non* of being a great, inspiring teacher. What is needed is the ability to pay attention to one's students. And Norris is exceptional at it.

For Norris, the operative word of the inner life is *renewal*. It's ironic that a sophisticated poet like her finds self-renewal in a

Catholic abbey. Catholics often don't recognize the richness they have to share with the rest of the world. Perhaps this current crisis will made us take stock by reexamining our faith, treasuring our nurturing traditions, and embracing a deep soul searching. Our American cardinals would perhaps be well advised to find the abbey Norris frequents to book a collective retreat. Let them seek out Norris's wise monk and have a heart-to-heart talk with him about how compassionately to address this scandal.

Art critic Bernard Berenson, a graduate of the school where I teach, observes that the greatest work of art of the Western world is the Catholic Church. He's not a cradle Catholic like his classmate George Santayana. According to his wife Mary, however, his conversion didn't take.

Berenson pursued art as if it was a religion, and it seemingly sufficed for him. Wallace Stevens did the same, but in the end he was baptized into the Church, a conversion that literary circles are loath to accept, as if Stevens were a deserter deserving to be shot.

As a teacher of literature, I identify with Norris's joy when kids "take" to poetry. By the time I get my students as upperclassmen, they've too often lost their interest in verse. They complain that poetry is "too hard to understand," especially the archaic language of Shakespeare, Shelley, Keats, or Wordsworth or that they've been coerced to memorize it, destroying any intrinsic joy. But every once in a while a miracle happens: a student is turned on by poetry, reading and even writing it. A moment for which every English teacher lives.

Today a student asks if she could recite for oratory a lyric by Britney Spears!

Norris writes at length about virginity. As a college student, she soon realizes that being a virgin is a rarity, and in the culture of Bennington, a risible one. She persists, however, in "protecting" herself, maintaining her distance from men by entering a "cloister" of reading. A classmate, however, takes a more drastic measure at freedom, mutilating her genitals to rid herself of a cruelly manipulative boyfriend.

Virginity and the Church. Celibacy and the priesthood. Homosexuality and the Church and the priesthood. Controversial issues when she was in college and they remain so today.

A nun remarks to Norris, "Virginity is a state that returns to God in wholeness. This wholeness is not that of having experienced all experiences, but of something reserved, preserved, or reclaimed for that it was made for. Virginity is the ability to stay centered, with oneness of purpose."[32]

Norris admires the nun's idealism, but she says that too often society has reduced women to an either/or status: she's either a whore or a nun. Having read Norris's last autobiographical book, *The Virgin of Bennington*, I'll reserve comment on this theme for later. But the idea that one isn't somehow "whole" after the loss of virginity or that virginity is a more "centered" state of being is one I consider unacceptable.

Being Christian, we are whole and centered in Christ. The physicality of remaining a virgin is a sacrifice, one freely offered to Christ, but it doesn't elevate a person to a higher level of physical or spiritual being. It's a gift freely given, with no strings attached; it isn't a fast lane to a deeper (higher) spirituality, as is often portrayed.

Norris explores virginity in political terms; she observes that women today can employ virginity as a tool to disrupt male authority and power.

Virginity as a gift and as a political tool: I must further explore.

Teaching the novel *Tess of the D'Urbervilles* is a difficult undertaking. My students haven't any patience with Hardy's long descriptive passages, and they also reject his pessimistic worldview. Young people need hope, and Hardy doesn't provide it.

Heck, we all need hope!

My students have nothing but disdain for the innocent and guileless Tess. One calls her a "sap." Another asks, "What's the big deal about being a virgin?" This is said in regard to Angel Clare's abandoning Tess when she confesses her own erotic past (and her child out of wedlock). Tess reveals her "sinful" past only after Angel admits his forty-eight hours of dissipation with a woman in London. Tess assumes that he'll understand and accept her youthful mistakes since he himself admits weakness. But she's dead wrong.

The ancient double standard!

A beautiful spring day although a bit on the cool side. Drove out to St. Joseph's Abbey, visiting the bookstore in search of Joan Chittister's book, *The Rule of Benedict*. They didn't have it, but I purchased another of hers on the Credo.

Benedict expected novices to enter his monastery not for his Rule, but for God. His Rule is a simple pointing of the finger toward the divine.

Came across a remarkable comment by Norris: "I had stumbled onto a basic truth of asceticism: that it is not necessarily a denigration of the body, though it has often been misapplied for that purpose. Rather, it is a way of surrendering to reduced circumstances in a manner that enhances the whole person."[33]

Her assessment of asceticism is astute. Too often the human body has been subjected to overzealous spirituality. Too often the body was flagellated, if not bruised, bloodied, or mutilated, as well as denied nutritious food and sound sleep—all in the name of God, as if God would be pleased to see us wounded, emaciated, and bone weary. Modern asceticism should be a matter of simplification or, as Norris says, of a reduction of matters interfering with developing a deeper relationship with God. And this applies not only to monks, but also to everyone. How much food, alcohol, sleep, work, TV, radio, and talk do we need? All of us could benefit from simplifying our lives. Henry David Thoreau recommends such a manner of lifestyle in *Walden* when he says "Simplify, simplify, simplify." Or perhaps he should have said it once: "Simplify!"

While serving as an artist-in-residence for the North Dakota Arts Council, Norris visits a number of schools throughout the state. She reads to her students, talks about being a poet herself, and encourages them to write their own poems. She receives from a girl an extraordinary description of the Dakota sky, "The sky is full of blue/and full of the mind of God."[34]

A gifted girl!

Norris writes about listening to the sky. I too find myself "listening" to the sky. My study window offers me a fine view of the sky to which I often give my attention. Today, for instance, it's a pale blue sky with small islands of cloud scudding over my house heading east toward the sea.

Norris says, "No one waits better than monks, or farmers."[35]
The act of waiting reminds me of Samuel Beckett's *Waiting for Godot*, Simone Weil's *Waiting for God*, and a verse from John Milton's poem "On His Blindness": "They also serve who only stand and wait."
Waiting is a spiritual way.

Who was the poet who said, "The meaning is the waiting"?

Torrential rain. The prediction is an inch of rain, but I can't complain for in this drought we need all the rain we can get. Just looked out my window and noticed how green my lawn is. Well, let the grass soak it in now because there might be a water ban this summer.
A verse from Gerard Manley Hopkins flies into memory, "Send my roots rain": his prayer isn't for literal rain but for God's grace to revive his dejected spirit. Hopkins, like both Norris and her husband, suffered from depression.

It's springtime, but it's snowing in Massachusetts! Still cold and the house heat still on. Yesterday torrential rains, and now snow. Oh well, we need it.

I enter a search engine with, "Rule of St. Benedict," and I'm surprised by the many Web sites devoted to it. I retrieve the Rule in many languages including Latin. One site, "Elements of Benedictine Life: A Way of Spiritual Development," begins with, "The Ideal: Above all, Benedictine life is aimed at seeking God. Everything in the Rule of St. Benedict is intended to facilitate this holy purpose." According to the site these are the elements of the Rule: stability, prayer, witness, *lectio divina*, celibacy, silence, obedience, community, poverty, renunciation, conversion, and work.

Later, I find a Web site devoted to defining a Benedictine Oblate. I discover that Dorothy Day and Paul Claudel as well as St. Thomas More and St. Thomas Becket had been oblates. I also discover that oblates don't take vows; they simply aspire to practice what St. Benedict taught; all this information found on a site called "Blue Cloud Abbey." A beautiful name!

Norris says poets are at the mercy of what they see. Yes, and that's why they must always be involved in a cleansing of the windows of the soul: to see better and to fine-tune their talent to describe what they see. Most of us don't see as acutely as poets, and we certainly don't have the verbal gifts necessary to create beautiful poems, and it's why we desperately need good poets: they wake us up and speak our own thoughts—the difference is that they express them poetically (i.e., beautifully).

We're fast approaching the end of the school year. Asking my students what they'll remember most about this year, they shout, "Epiphany!" I'm often on the lookout for "moments of epiphany" in our study of literature.

In our first classes, I had explained to them that epiphany is a moment of self-realization associated with the fiction of James Joyce. When Joyce began his career as a novelist, he kept a notebook recording moments charged with a heightened significance. In 1904–45, Joyce used the term *epiphany* for the first time in his first novel *Stephen Hero*, defining epiphany as a "spiritual manifestation."

Critics have co-opted epiphany and today it refers to a character's achieving life-changing self-knowledge, an event compared to the Epiphany, the feast of the Magi visiting the Christ child, because to gaze upon the Christ child was for the Magi the supreme revelation.

Norris encourages her students to write about their epiphanic moments. Verse is, of course, the perfect medium to capture such wondrous moments. There's the girl who wrote, "When my third snail died, I said, 'I'm through with snails.'" Later, impressed by the girl's comment, Norris incorporates it in a poem,

When my third snail died, I said,
"I'm through with snails."
But I didn't mean it.[36]

Universal wisdom: After a disappointment, we often say we're giving up but then find ourselves still pushing ahead through and beyond our failures, proof of the indomitable human spirit.

When my class and I analyze fiction or verse, we search for moments of insight. Our searching is a paradigm for their own pursuit of self-knowledge—or rather, I hope it is. Their attempt at *explication de texte* is an effort to penetrate the mystery of a literary work, but it may also lead to their own efforts to penetrate the mystery of their own being.

It's rather late in the academic year for *Hamlet*, but we must read and study it because it's a required text. It's almost impossible to teach *Hamlet* without referring to Catholic theology. Two examples prove my point. The famous "To Be or Not To Be" soliloquy is a meditation on suicide. I point out to my students that to take or not to take one's life is a moral dilemma for Hamlet. He is unhappy and troubled; he has lost his joy in living and death seems to be an escape "devoutly to be wished for."[37] What prevents him from killing himself is his Catholic conscience (it's likely that Shakespeare was a cradle Catholic). Suicide is contrary to his religion, and the consequence is eternal damnation (the belief at that time): "Thus conscience does make cowards of us all."[38] To exchange a temporary "sea of troubles" for an eternity in hell doesn't appear to be a fair exchange to the young Hamlet; thus, he opts to endure and to live, aligning himself with the theology/morality of the time.

Not only does Norris encourage students to write verse but she also helps them to get in touch with what is important within their souls. A Native American girl loves to write poems, and Norris praises her for them, "You must love to write." The girl shifts from one foot to another and says, "I don't have paper at home so I keep them in my head. That's where they live until I write them down."[39]

What an extraordinary encounter: an established artist and a budding poet. The girl, I wager, will never forget the day she met Kathleen Norris.

Second example: Hamlet has yet to avenge his father's death. His dilatory measures are beginning to plague him (he fears he's a coward). On his way to confront his mother in her chamber, he by chance encounters King Claudius on his knees praying. This is his best opportunity thus far to kill the solitary and unguarded Claudius. Hamlet says,

> Now might I do it pat
> Now he is a-praying
> And now I'll do it. (He draws his sword)[40]

He instantly perceives the theological implications: Killing Claudius while he is praying may send him to heaven:

> And so he goes to heaven
> And so am I revenged.
> That would be scanned:
> A villain kills my father, and for that,
> I, his sole son, do the same villain send
> To heaven.[41]

Hamlet's worldview is imbued with Catholicism; he understands full well that any sinner, even a murderer like Claudius, guilty of regicide and incest, can win heaven by an act of genuine contrition—somehow I must convey this import to my students.

Norris recounts the teacher whose administrator ordered him not to teach Shakespeare, "the kids don't need it."[42] I run into the same argument from parents. "What good will Shakespeare do urban kids?" a father once asked me.

One might as well ask, "What good is beauty?"

What good is the Rule of St. Benedict in the twenty-first century? To understand its relevance, Norris reads Esther de Waal, a student of Benedictine spirituality. De Waal writes,

> I find that Benedict touches us all because he shows such a deep grasp of the human psyche. He writes out of this sense of who we are and where we are on our human journey. This can only come from his own experience. He recognizes the deepest of all human needs: the need for order, inner and outer, the need to love and be loved, and above all the need to be at home in all the many levels of meaning that the word can carry.[43]

Weather is still cool, and today frost sparkling on the windshield. On May 21! Warm weather is promised for the Memorial Day weekend. This week senior classes read poetry: James Wright, Linda Pastan, and Robinson Jeffers.

Norris teaches poetry to grammar school children; I teach juniors and seniors. Teaching younger children, I believe, is easier: they rarely have prejudice toward poetry. Nevertheless, my students and I have some interesting discussions about poems. They especially liked Linda Pastan's "Woman Holding a Balance, Vermeer, 1664" and James Wright's "Lying in a Hammock at William Duffy's Farm in Pine Island, Minnesota."

The artist Vermeer has always been special to me. In the late 1960s and early 1970s I became friends with the first woman to teach at Boston Latin School, an all male school founded in 1635. She was an art teacher of great talent. We often visited the Gardner Museum located behind our school. Before she'd look at anything else, Diane would head for the second floor to gaze upon Vermeer's *The Concert*, her favorite painting. How angry and sad she was when in the famous heist of 1990, this painting (along with ten others) was stolen. And have yet to be found.

Our visits to the Gardener were the beginning of my love for Vermeer's work. I've traveled to New York's Frick Museum and the Metropolitan, and the Rijksmuseum in Amsterdam for the privilege of standing before his radiant distillations of time sanctified. In the silent ambience of museums I found peace. I don't remember who said it, but I agree with it: Beautiful art leads the viewer to peace.

Kathleen Norris also seeks peace, discovering it not in a museum but in the silent ambience of a Benedictine abbey. Abbeys and museums aren't so very different; both demand finely tuned powers of attention, the former directed toward *lectio divina* and the latter toward the visual arts.

Attention isn't a passive activity; rather, it is the mustering of our whole self to be focused on something *other*. And then, paradoxically, we forget our self in the act of attending.

To foster my students' understanding of Linda Pastan's poem "Woman Holding a Balance, Vermeer, 1664" I bring to class a reproduction of Vermeer's famous painting. As a preface to our discussion, I share with them my trip to Washington, DC, in

1995 to visit the National Gallery where twenty-one of the thirty-five extant Vermeer paintings were on exhibit. I had stood before "Woman Holding a Balance" for a long time. I read to them what I'd written about that moment:

As a woman gently lifts a balance in her right hand, pearls and gold on the table shine in the sunlight streaming through a window. She is dressed in a blue coat edged in white ermine and wears a veil on her head. Her face is so lovely and contemplative that I am reminded of the Blessed Mother. I remember Vermeer converted to Catholicism and wonder if he was influenced by the importance of Mary in Catholic iconography and ritual. Behind the woman is a painting of the Last Judgment. Vermeer's exhortation is obvious: It is the final weighing of our soul that is important. Our soul is the pearl of great price.[44]

Then we read Pastan's poem,

The picture within
the picture is The Last
Judgement, subdued
as wallpaper in the background.
And though the woman
holding the scales
is said to be weighing
not a pearl or a coin
but the heft of a single soul,
this hardly matters.

It is really the mystery
of the ordinary
we're looking at—the way
Vermeer has sanctified the light
the same light that enters
our own grimed windows
each morning, touching
a cheek, the fold
of a dress, a jewelry box
with perfect justice.[45]

My class of juniors enjoyed the poem. Here are a few of their insights,

"There's nothing on the scales; consequently, no one is being
judged."
"The grimed windows represent our daily way of seeing so
that we don't often see the 'mystery of the ordinary.'"
"Sunlight is not judgmental; therefore, it shines on everything equally."
"Perhaps at the end of the world the 'perfect justice' will be
unconditional forgiveness."

I'm pleased by their mature, insightful remarks, uttered in a public school where to discuss spiritual issues is problematic, to say the least.

Judgment is one of those Christian words Norris has come to terms with in her book *Amazing Grace: A Vocabulary of Faith.* The language of faith, she feels, creates a gap between herself and belief because words like *faith*, *dogma*, *salvation*, *sinner*, and *judgment* have become a "scary vocabulary," language so burdened with codified or abstract connotations that their original meaning is almost impenetrable. In short, theological language needs to be purged; otherwise, people, especially the young, are turned off religion. Or intimidated by it.

For instance, she comments on the parable of the weeds and the wheat in Matthew 13,

> I began to find the parable absurdly freeing not from the responsibility but from the disease of perfectionism. Even the image of fire, which had troubled me so as a child, was transformed into a symbol of hope....I began to see God's fire, like a good parent's righteous anger, as something that can flare up, challenge, and even change us, but that does not destroy the essence of who we are. The thought of all my weeds burning off so that only the wheat remains came to seem a good thing.[46]

As a poet she is naturally supersensitive to words and feels she must somehow reclaim religious language as her birthright. Reclamation lies in seeing words again with rinsed eyes. Rereading the Gospel with absolute attention, she examines words the way Pastan gazed upon Vermeer's painting, hoping to penetrate the "mystery of the ordinary."[47]

Rereading the parable of the weeds and wheat in such a deconstructive fashion, Norris wins new interpretation as well as personal, spirit-enhancing revelation.

My students are intrigued by James Wright's poem, "Lying in a Hammock," especially its last line when he says, "I have wasted my life."[48] We had a deep discussion about what he meant: We conclude that a life without an appreciation of beauty is a wasted one. I remind them that they themselves are reading and diligently delving more deeply into beautiful verse. "Your lives are not wasted," I say. They wanly smile.

Today we read in class Norris's poem "Eve of St. Agnes in the High School Gym." I look forward to reading their opinions.

> The saint's been dead too long;
> no young girl keeps her vigil.
> Not one fasts
> or prays tonight, for a vision
> of the one she'll marry.
>
> A band plays—too loudly—
> popular tunes a few years out-of-date.
> Young men emerge from a huddle
> of teammates, cheerleaders,
> fans. They run onto the court,
> howling, slapping hands.
>
> Men just a few years older
> stand smoking by the door;
> their windbreakers advertise a local bar.
> Others sit in the stands,

holding sleepy children;
the women with them look worried and tired.

Snow falls silently,
Snaking through the streets,
While in the gym, done up like spring
In a pale yellow skirt
And lavender sweater,
A pretty girl sleepwalks
on high heels. She carries herself
To a boy on the bench
who doesn't look up; and the old men sigh.

When the game is over
they flee on the storm.
The saint sits in heaven,
and if anyone's praying
on this chilly night,
let it be for love.[49]

Students pick up on the ennui of the lives of almost everyone
in the gym and the lack of love in their lives. They comment on
the girls who don't need to pray to St. Agnes for a vision of their
future husbands because as natives of a small town they more
often than not marry their high school classmates, boys they often
don't love, thus repeating their parents' lives of quiet desperation,
along with babies, bills, and low-paying jobs.

One student describes the poem as sad, for everyone in the
poem "sleepwalks," like the girl walking toward a boy who refuses

to look up at her. There's no magic in their lives, she explains, because they accept a life of conditioning, habit, and routine.

One of my best students, a quiet, thoughtful young man, personalizes his essay,

> The lack of love and persistent loneliness of characters keeps them from transcending barriers placed upon them by their society. In urging a quest for love, Norris speaks to me in many aspects. I constantly feel the need to find love within my life, be it in the air, the trees, or the people I connect with daily. It's love for life which drives me daily, a love for all that's new and original, and all that's plain and antiquated. I believe Norris displays in this poem a void...she provides a springboard which we ought to use to delve into our own psyches and question our own realities. Are we living to our potential and seeking a love which may help guide our lives?

Such a commentary makes teaching worthwhile.

"Eve of St. Agnes" is a religious poem, or, rather, it's spiritual, one young adults can identify with, and it should be anthologized in high school texts. Unfortunately, Norris hasn't yet received the recognition she deserves as a poet. Part of the reason is that her nonfiction has been so enormously popular it's obscured her books of verse.

I had assigned for homework W. H. Auden's poem "Musée des Beaux Arts," concerning Breugel's painting about the myth of

Icarus. We read it aloud. I then called upon a student to explain the consequences of Icarus's failure to obey his father's warning not to fly too close to the sun.

"The wax of his wings would melt," she says, "and he'd fall to his death."

"Icarus's death was caused by his failure to be attentive to his father's admonition?" I ask.

After a long pause, she reluctantly says, "I guess so." She's obviously on Icarus's side.

The Icarus myth is often taught as an example of Greek didacticism. Christians present it as an exemplum of the sin of pride. But many Boston Latin School students don't relate to the word *sin*—it means little if anything to them.

Sin is one of those words Norris reclaims. And she allows no dillydallying about it; she confesses, "I am a sinner."[50]

Norris writes about *lectio divina* ("holy reading"). She considers it a means toward enhancing one's life in faith. If only my kids could see reading poetry as *holy* reading, whose value is incalculable, my job would then be easier. They need to be converted. But how?

When the word *grace* appears in the text of *Macbeth*, I ask my students for a definition. No one raises a hand and many sitting in front of me are confirmed Catholics. "Have you ever heard of 'sanctifying grace?'" I ask. No one responds.

A cool spring day. Last night much thunder, lightning, and torrential rains. No one complains about the rain; our drought-plagued New England thirsts for it.

An uneasy night. I watch the news with its coverage of fighting between India and Pakistan and the possibility of nuclear employment. Shades of the Cuban missile crisis when I was in high school, another night I couldn't sleep.

All one can do is pray for peace.

I enjoy reading Norris's *Little Girls in Church*. None of her poems can be described as political, unlike another poet I admire, Denise Levertov, who penned many political poems, perhaps too many. Norris addresses the plight of modern women searching for belief. She also writes of her life growing up: interior poems with a Vermeer-like light.

I particularly like her poem "Perennials."

I've betrayed them all:
columbine and daisy,
iris, day-lily,
even the rain barrel
that spoke to me in a dream.

I inherited this garden,
and miss my grandmother
in her big sun hat.
My inexperienced hands
don't know what to hope for.

Still, flowers come: yellow,
pink, and blue. Preoccupied

I let them go
until weeds produce spikes
and seeds around them.

I never used the rain barrel.
Water froze in the bottom;
too late, I set it on its side.

Now lily-of-the-valley comes
with its shy bloom,
choked by a weed
I don't know the name of. One day,
too late, I'll weed around them,
and pull some lilies by mistake.

Next year we'll all be back,
struggling.

Just look at these flowers
I've done nothing to deserve:
and still, they won't abandon me.[51]

She employs a garden as a metaphor for life, a familiar one in literature from Shakespeare to Vaughn to Voltaire to modern poets like R. M. Rilke, T. S. Eliot, Theodore Roethke, and James Wright.

Norris inherits her grandmother's garden, and not being a gardener, she's unsure about what to do with it. But she'll learn by going where she has to go. Even when she's doing nothing (*we wei*, meaning "doing nothing," is a Chinese philosophy), the flowers still bloom, the trees leaf, and the weeds sprout.

Like another gardener/poet, Emily Dickinson, Norris is more faithful than she knows, relishing the loveliness of her garden: the columbine, daisy, day-lily, and so on. Thus as a poet she succeeds: her attention is riveted to beauty—the vocation of a poet.

Even weeds have a right to exist, and next year will undoubtedly return.

Gardening and spirituality: we try to become beautiful souls, and if we succeed it's not because we've conquered our sins (weeds) but more likely because we've received the grace that, as the poem says, we've "done nothing to deserve." And we know that God never abandons us, ever faithful to us as are the perennial flowers he created.

Norris observes that nearly every Dickinson poem contains a reference to scripture, the Bible known if not adhered to. Dickinson writes to her cousin, "Consider the lilies is the only commandment I ever obeyed."

And if we truly see with our total being, it's the only commandment we need obey, the others falling in line.

A windy, sunny day. I spend part of the morning at the Museum of Fine Arts (MFA), attending the Impressionist Still Life Exhibit. Some of my favorite painters are showcased: Van Gogh, Manet, Cassatt, Cézanne, and Monet.

I'm glad to attend the exhibit while I'm reading Norris. After reading Norris's constant reminders to herself to pay strict attention, particularly to the meaning of the psalms, I find the quality of own attention is sharper.

Concerning attention, Norris quotes favorite poet William Stafford,

> A quality of attention has been given to you:
> When you turn your head the whole world
> Leans forward. It waits there thirsting
> After its names, and you speak it all out
> As it comes to you.[52]

At the Impressionist exhibit at the MFA, I imagine artists whispering from their framed paintings, "Pay attention." So I attend their pictures of flowers, fish, apples, plums, grapes, peaches, birds' nests, sleeping children, ladies drinking tea, and crystal goblets sparkling with wine. My eyes tenderly touch each painting. On departing, I feel I've done my soul good: my eyes having looked and listened well.

A beautiful day with a soft blue sky. After three days of rain (2.3 inches of rain has helped to relieve our drought), I'm happy to see the return of the sun. While my bird companions chant outside the window, I fortify myself with a cup of Maxwell Lite coffee, ready to embark upon the day's work.

Received an e-mail from Alibris.com: My order of Philip Toynbee's diaries is now on its way; it will take about a week to arrive from England. Richard Whitfield—who knew Toynbee—

ommended the diaries. At my recommendation, he had read the diaries of Loran Hurnscot and as a sort of *quid pro quo*, he said that I would enjoy Toynbee's similar spiritual journey, one fraught with spiritual ups and downs ultimately leading him to the peace of a Benedictine abbey.

What a pleasure it is to receive longed-for books in the mail: the anticipation, the tearing open of the package, the scrupulous unpacking, the gradual emergence of the book's cover, then the title, the exploration for damage, and finally to hold it lovingly in one's hands. Then the hope that what's within its covers may transform one's thinking or perhaps one's life.

Not many pleasures equal it.

Padre Pio is declared a saint. I know little about Padre Pio except that he was a stigmatic and possessed paranormal powers like bilocation. But yesterday I received a letter from a woman in Essex, England. She'd read my book on Merton and wished to share her thoughts. Inside the letter was a Padre Pio prayer card. Such synchronicities mystify me.

The school year is almost over, and I can then devote more time to Kathleen Norris. I haven't yet begun to reread her memoir *The Virgin of Bennington*. I was disappointed on my first reading: she wrote too little about herself, devoting too much space to her mentor Betty Kray. But I'm sure I'll gain new insights on a second reading. One of its highlights is her encounters with many poets: Jim Carroll, Denise Levertov, James Merrill, James Wright, and Stanley Kunitz. Interesting to me because I teach their poems.

I attend a poetry reading whose star attraction was the poet Robert Pinsky (former poet laureate and founder of the *Favorite Poems* books); I haven't read much of his verse. I'm aware of his translation of Dante's *Inferno*, but I've no desire to read it, having already read several fine translations including John Ciardi's excellent one.

Louise Glück (American poet laureate) steals the show with her beautiful, deeply felt reading of George Herbert's poem "Love, iii." I'm quite moved. She then reads one of her own poems. She's a lovely woman with an elegant speaking voice, worth the trip to see and to hear her.

Is Kathleen Norris a good poetry reader?

Cloudless sky, in the 70s, dry air, and clear sunlight all add up to a beautiful June day. School's out for the summer! I have many plans, but my top priority is to finish my walk with Kathleen Norris.

Summer

≋ ≋

Attention Is a Genuflection to the Moment

In *The Virgin of Bennington* Norris praises Denise Levertov as
an excellent reader of poetry. Norris says she herself started out as
a poor reader but improved with time and by listening to good
readers like Levertov. She says, "A reading by Denise Levertov was
for me a seminar in how to do it right. I was thrilled to hear a poet
I had found on my own in high school."[53]

After flirting with Christianity for much of her adulthood,
Levertov embraces it at the end of her life. It took great courage to
become a Catholic, for she knew full well that her decision could
be "suicide" in today's intellectual milieu. And yet wherever she
read, she packed the place with poetry lovers of every generation.

When I wrote to her several years back to ask her if she had
discovered Lady Julian of Norwich (she has written two beautiful
poems about Julian) through Thomas Merton, she immediately
responded by letter, explaining that she'd known about Lady
Julian long before she met Merton at the Abbey of Gethsemani in
Kentucky (he admired her verse); she added that she respected
Merton's verse but in no way was influenced by him.

If anything, Merton may have been influenced by Levertov.

Norris's description of Denise Levertov,

And then Levertov took the stage. By the time she finished one poem, I felt as if I had been refreshed by a glass of cool water. To employ a phrase Betty sometimes used to explain why people go to poetry readings, it was the relief of hearing language again after so much verbiage. No clever surfaces here, but only words that mattered, words with authority. No longer did I feel merely a passive witness to a poet's vanity. Levertov brought the world in, and allowed me in as well, and the darkened auditorium became a sacred space, a place of prayer and meditation. She made me aware that a poetry reading could be an act of generosity to an audience, to which anyone might respond with the whole heart.[54]

What a tribute!

I am well into Joan Chittister's *The Rule of Benedict: Insights for the Ages*. St. Benedict says,

Your way of acting should be different from the world's way; the love of Christ must come before all else. You are not to act in anger or nurse a grudge. Rid your heart of all deceit. Never give a hollow greeting of peace or turn away when someone needs your love. Bind yourself to no oath lest it prove false, but speak the truth with heart and tongue.[55]

Chittister's analysis of this passage cuts to the very heart of the Benedictine way of life when she says, "The end of Benedictine spirituality is to develop a transparent personality. Dissimulation, half answers, vindictive attitudes, a false presentation of self are all barbs in the soul of the monastic."[56]

Benedict advocates that we be ourselves: We are not to pretend, not to be two-faced, not to be deceitful. It's exactly what draws Norris to his Rule: she needs to be herself; she needs to reach out to people for authentic contact. Perhaps her attraction to teaching children about poetry satisfies a need to be around the mask-less, dissembling being foreign to children. Norris knows plenty about dissembling, learning well its lessons at Bennington College, and New York City where it's a way of life—as well as a legitimate survival technique.

Philip Toynbee's two diaries, *Part of a Journey* and *End of a Journey* have arrived from England. Like Norris, Toynbee was a searcher, and like her, he found peace of soul at a Benedictine abbey. He was very moved by the nuns' chanting of the psalms. The psalms themselves, however, were problematic for him. He writes,

> Evensong at Tymawr. Holy and loving sisters singing the psalms. Because St. Benedict started the practice 1400 years ago. And this antiquity of the tradition is impressive. But what contortions of mind and heart must be needed to convert so much brazen self-righteousness, so much whining self-pity, so much bloodthirsty vindictiveness into a "type" of Christ's passion—or whatever meaning they give it.[57]

I agree with him. But I also agree with Norris who says the psalms, to be useful, have to be read psychologically. In the psalms,

I see my own self-righteousness, my whining self-pity and, yes, my tendency to be vindictive. The psalms serve as a mirror of my shadow; thus, if I'm sufficiently attentive, I may achieve a deeper self-knowledge, and on that level anyone can relate to the psalms.

Let's not forget that the psalms are also some of the most beautiful poems ever written. And Norris, a published poet, and Toynbee a *poet manqué*, would both appreciate the beautiful, powerful imagery as well as the lyricism of the psalms.

Concerning the prevalence of anger throughout the psalms, Norris writes,

> The anger of God speaks the truth. No matter how "nice" we think we are, or morally in the right, our hands, too, are full of blood; we do not exist as little kingdoms apart from our human societies full of murder, thievery, cheating, whole systems of oppression. I have come to have a certain level of trust in God's anger; it is a response to what is genuinely wrong.[58]

Today arrives a letter from the English poet Kathleen Raine. She has a box of letters by English novelist/diarist Gay Taylor (a.k.a. Loran Hurnscot). She writes,

> I have a whole boxful of her [Gay's] letters to her close lifelong friend the writer Malachy Whittaker. They corresponded at great length. I have no letters from Gay myself, I probably had a few but did not keep letters, and our relation [sic] was in any case conversational rather than by letter. She left me many of her books, including Indian texts and Yeats' A Vision. I would

be very grateful if you would do something about editing Gay's letters—I am ninety-four now and cant [sic] undertake it, and I had my own work to do....Far too many to photocopy you would really have to come to England and see what there is and take them away.[59]

What an offer! I'd love to write a commentary on Hurnscot's diary, *A Prison: A Paradise*. She is the Lady Julian of the twentieth century but may have to wait a long time before she's discovered. If I could help to promote her cause, I'd be proud and willing.

But a trip to London is out of the question at this time. Perhaps Richard Whitfield will serve as my proxy.

The beginning of Norris's third autobiographical volume, *The Virgin of Bennington*, is rather moving. Norris had gone to live in Honolulu when she was in the seventh grade. She couldn't penetrate the solidarity of her classmates who'd attended school together since kindergarten; consequently, she was a lonely child, retreating to books and music for solace. Her mother was a teacher, her father a cellist, so it's no wonder books and music became her refuge.

As a young teenager of the 1960s, she was precocious, reading Kierkegaard and seeing Ingmar Bergman's movies alone. She chose to attend Bennington College because it was a women's college where she could "study free of the distractions and social failures I had endured in a coed high school."[60]

At an early age, she had clearly embarked on a spiritual journey. In both Kierkegaard and Bergman, she caught glimpses that would, as Wordsworth would say, "make life less forlorn." And yet the perspective of these northern souls is darkly existential, questionable soul-food for a teenager.

A week on the Cape near water proves to be exactly what I needed, and I've returned home rejuvenated.

In the meantime, our third heat wave has transmogrified my lawn into hay. No rain and no prediction of rain in the near future. There's currently no water ban in Boston so I'm prodigiously watering the lawn, hoping to re-green it.

"Water" for our souls: silence, solitude, and beauty, both of liturgy and of nature. Time on the Cape provides all three.

Norris's poem, "The Companionable Dark" is stunningly beautiful. It addresses the theme of the "dark night of the soul" as does my new novel, *The Exquisite Risk*. My character Paula Young explains what John of the Cross means by his expression "dark night of the soul." She says,

> Today we often misuse John of the Cross's mystical expression "dark night" to describe a number of things, especially depression. But it refers to a specific phase of the spiritual journey. The mystic who finds herself in a dark night is stripped of everything: of the presence of God, of consolation in prayer, of certainty, and of peace. She simply surrenders to what is, faithfully waiting.[61]

In "The Companionable Dark," Norris refers to several different kinds of darkness: the "companionable dark," the "brooding dark," the "faithful dark," the "deep down dark," "the dark in which stars burn," the "dark by which we see," the "dark like truth" and the "dark of a needle's eye."

She doesn't refer to the darkest darkness: the dark of total abandonment, a state of utter loneliness: "My God, my God, why have you forsaken me?" (Mark 15:34).

Norris fell into promiscuity as a college student. After a love affair with a young woman, she subsequently enters an affair with a married male professor.

As a young person of the 1960s' counter-revolution, she lived when traditional sexual mores were being challenged and often discarded. With new revelations about the priest scandal hitting our newspapers everyday—new allegations against an archbishop in Australia and another priest here in Boston—her experiences are comparatively "innocent." I respect her for sharing such intimate information. She didn't have to.

Since the publication of *The Cloister Walk* in 1996, Norris has achieved tremendous credibility as a spokesperson for contemporary spiritual life, and her willingness to describe how lost and alienated she was in her youth is a testament to an admirable integrity. To write about one's blunders demands courage and when they are of a sexual nature, it requires a daring humility.

Fall

∾ ∾

Attention Is the Soul's Sunbeam

I return to school with a different attitude: it's my last year of teaching, and I don't feel the usual pressures of a new academic year. The old maxim "And this too will pass" is not just an adage but nearly a reality.

I'm happy to see the students. There is something life-enhancing about young people so full of energy, intelligence, and potential.

Willa Cather's *My Antonia* is my juniors' first book for reading and study. The foreword is coincidentally written by Kathleen Norris. She comments on how risky it had been for Cather to write about ordinary people, predominantly European immigrants: Czechs, Swedes, Norwegians, and Germans. She says Cather would today be fascinated by the new influx of Asian and Hispanic immigrants now enriching our land, and she would've avidly read the books they'll eventually write about their assimilation.

Norris is herself a risk taker: she not only writes about the American landscape but she also honestly describes the arid, contemporary American soulscape. Rejecting secular society, she finds herself returning to traditional values, ones that America had discarded in the second half of the twentieth century: value·

like silence, solitude, reading the Bible, listening for the "still, small voice" of God.

Reading *My Antonia*, I'm overwhelmed by Cather's descriptions of the beauty of Nebraska. Through Jim Burden's eyes, I see his first glimpse of Nebraska, "There was nothing but land: not a country at all, but the material out of which countries are made."[62]

While composing *Dakota*, Norris recognizes in the wide, solitary spaces of midwestern landscape and skyscape her need for space, silence, and solitude: the material of which souls are made.

Landscape as a means of spiritual restoration: Wordsworth discovered this truth, his opus a testament devoted to it. Here in America, Thoreau also wrote about nature's powers of rejuvenation. And today there are a number of poets singing the praises of nature's beauty: Mary Oliver, Jane Kenyon, and Charles Wright.

Even Thomas Merton finally understood the importance of nature, and during his final days living in his hermitage, he spent much time gazing upon the trees, hills, sky, and animals around him. And their descriptions are some of his finest writing. Nature became his *lectio divina*.

When God is seemingly absent in her life, Norris turns to people or landscape: both are *loci Dei*.

As a Benedictine oblate, Norris practices *lectio divina*, contemplatively reading the psalms and the New Testament. But she insists on sharing the fruit of holy reading with her brothers and sisters. She writes,

> All this meandering through the text, and my personal reflections on it, does not remain private if I employ it in a sermon to help others find themselves in the story, or even if I use it to remind myself to be more charitable to the Marthas and the Marys that I meet.[63]

How amazing that people in the twenty-first century still center their lives around St. Benedict's Rule, accepting its universal wisdom. I'm astonished by the number of books that have been recently published about Benedictine spirituality. Who would've thought that Americans, passionate about freedom, would submit themselves to a rule, and an ancient one at that?

Norris's *lectio divina* at Bennington is poetry. Reading it became a passion for her: "it appeared to be a way of life."[64] Like many a college freshman, she approaches understanding poetry as one would tackle a math problem: it must be solved. After her professor encourages her to write verse, she starts to pen her own poems and never looks back.

Under the aegis of Betty Kray, she works for the Academy of American Poets and hears and meets many of the best poets writing; thus, she learns to recognize good poetry. She lauds poets like Louise Bogan and James Merrill who both offered her sound advice about writing verse. When she's a college senior, she reads and falls in love with James Wright's verse, particularly *The Branch Will Not Break* and *Shall We Gather at the River* which "shook her to the core."[65] After reading Wright, she knows the kind of poetry she wanted to write.

James Wright won the Pulitzer Prize for poetry in 1972. This year, 2004, his son Franz Wright won it. How proud his father would be if he were alive. His son is also a convert to Catholicism, his poetry charting his journey into the church.

Norris is only six years older than Franz (b. 1953), and she surely must've known him when he was a young man. I wonder if they discussed poetry, or perhaps have shared their poetry.

Norris came to know James Wright and his wife Anne through the American Academy. When the poet went to Europe, Norris sublet his apartment.

She also volunteered to type his manuscripts, an activity that taught her much about verse making, particularly about rhythm and rhyme. If she made a mistake typing, she'd type the page over; this way Wright's verse became second nature to her.

The dominant theme of Wright's poetry is the journey motif. He longed for a return to innocence, to the state of man before the fall. His favorite poets were Edward Thomas and Horace.

Norris too searches for innocence and the kingdom of heaven.

Poetry offers meaning to Norris's life. Even an anti-Vietnam War rally in Washington, DC, couldn't keep her away from a poetry contest at Mount Holyoke College where she tied for second place.

Fortunate not to fall into drug or alcohol addiction, she fell into poetry. If one is to fall into anything, let it be poems: they erved as her safety net.

Poetry has for years been my refuge, certain verses serving as talismans helping me through many an ordeal.

Favorite poems have lifted my spirits, dispersing the depression or despair vying for my soul. A simple phrase will do it, like the time I read Eliot's *Four Quartets* and first came across Lady Julian's promise that "All things shall be well." What tears of joy when I read her words!

My memory fingers verses the way others finger "worry beads."

One could say poetry was Norris's "religion" but it's truer to say that poetry led her to religion.

Richard Whitfield has kindly agreed to pick up Gay Taylor's archives at Kathleen Raine's London home and to deliver them to me here in Boston. I'm thrilled. I've also promised her to find a home for the archives in a New England college, one with a Women's Studies program. (Note: they are now housed at Boston's Simmons College.)

Gay Taylor was a published novelist, diarist, and book reviewer; she married Hal Taylor, founder of the famous Golden Cockerel Press, and her friends were some of the twentieth century's most well-known writers: Kathleen Raine, David Gascoyne, A. E. Coppard, Willa and Edwin Muir, Antonia White, and many others. She is one of the great spiritual diarists of the last century, one I hope will be widely known someday.

In *The Virgin of Bennington* there is little mention of formal religion. Norris's college life is completely secular. She bluntly says, "I had deemed the Christian religion useless baggage, having no place in my sophisticated life. But I was aware that I needed something, and the way I had been living, pursuing an exotic nightlife and casual, one-night sexual encounters with friends no longer seemed the way to find it."[66]

Norris and I were born in 1947. At college she saw lots of drugs and sex, while I saw little of it. But we both, it seems, were very much aware of the Vietnam War and the angry dissatisfaction among people of our generation.

In my senior year of college, I turned to a study of Buddhism, seeking a deeper spirituality, one fostering meditation and enlightenment. Weary of churchy didacticism, I said to a friend that if I heard one more sermon on mortal sin and the eternal fires of hell, I'd renounce religion forever.

I read Alan Watts, D. Suzuki, Christmas Humphreys, Aldous Huxley, and Herman Hesse. I also discovered Carl Jung, and spent ten years reading and studying him. Poetry seriously entered my life after studying with Helen Vendler at Boston University (she's now at Harvard) and Paul Mariani at the University of Massachusetts, Amherst (he's now at Boston College). They are two excellent teachers and brilliant critics, the latter also a fine poet.

Norris found sustenance in poetry, and later in the Rule of St. Benedict and the psalms.

Norris's star poets' list at the American Academy of Poetry is quite impressive: Donald Justice, Isabelle Gardner, Thom Gunn, David Hoffman, Theodore Roethke, Karl Shapiro, Allen Tate, and Richard Wilbur.

To come in contact with such poetic luminaries must have been heaven for the budding young poet, and some, like James Merrill, offered her sound advice about verse making, particularly how to break a line.

When Norris was in high school, she carried in her book-bag, not a Bible but the poetry of Alan Ginsberg and Denise Levertov. Ginsberg is the heir of Whitman and Levertov, as I see it, the heir of Emily Dickinson. Not bad reading for a teenager: the child is mother of the woman.

From Betty Kray, Norris learns that verse is meant to be heard, and it was Kray more than anyone in America who pushed for poetry readings, insisting that to experience the wonder of poetry, one must hear it.

The Virgin of Bennington: the title of chapter five: "Salvation by Poetry."[67]
The chapter title says it all.

Today a brief letter from Kathleen Raine; she writes,

By all means tell Richard Whitfield to get in touch with me about her letters. It is an ideal plan.[68]

She trusts Richard because they both share royal sponsorship. All these synchronicities are spooky!

Like Norris, my friend Peggy Rosenthal (author of *The Poets' Jesus*) turns to poetry in time of need. Her book *Praying through Poetry: Hope for Violent Times* just arrived today. She writes,

In the numbness after September 11, 2001, I found that only the arts could lift my spirit. I craved classical music and went to concert after concert throughout the fall. I'd take an afternoon off to go and sit in front of a painting in the museum, planting myself on the floor and letting my gaze soak in the art and be soaked in by it. And, especially, I read and meditated with poetry, grateful for the way its language and imagery "reach comfortably into experience"—as poet Naomi Shihab Nye has said—"holding and connecting it more successfully than any news channel we could name."[69]

Peggy and I have discussed poetry's affinity to prayer, agreeing that the source of both verse and prayer is the Holy Spirit.

Norris's account of Betty's Kray's death of cancer is touching and inspiring. Her heart failed just as she was to begin a final round of chemotherapy. The last thing Betty said to Norris was "Don't let your monks forget about me."[70]

Norris's poem "Ignominy of the Living" is a tribute to her mentor Betty Kray. It's not so much elegiac as humorous: Norris remembers her dear friend as a person always smiling. That alone is tribute to the kind of person she was.

Another poem I like is "The Tolling" about the death of another friend, Brother Louis, who also wrote verse. She admires his poetry because it's "clean and spare."[71] Reading through *Journey: New and Selected Poems, 1969–1999*, I notice that Norris's verse becomes cleaner and leaner. It's as if the monastic ideal of diminishment influences every area of life, including her poetic aesthetic, and it's most obvious in the last poems of *Journey*.

Less is more, a lesson I learned while writing novels.

A fine example of her spare verse is "Body and Soul," an exquisite lyric about attention. She identifies with Jesus, the Man of Sorrow, but even though she is "stupid with worry," she stops to admire "the weedy hollyhocks/by a neighbor's backyard fence."[72] Her attention to beauty even amidst suffering (her husband's stricken with cancer) is a consolation. She drinks in the world's beauty as the bumblebee drinks in "the milk of the world."

Asked about how to deal with anxiety, Christ says, "Behold the lilies of the field." We spare ourselves anxiety when we shift our attention from ourselves to focus it on something other. The simplicity of such wisdom is astonishing.

When Norris turned to religion, Kray feared her poetry would become didactic. Although Norris rejects preachiness, she indeed becomes more religious and allusively Christian. There aren't too many modern poems with references to Jesus, the Agnus Dei, and St. Thérèse.

Betty Kray believed in the spiritual dimension of writing verse. Norris writes,

Betty believed that writing poetry could lead you through all the vicissitudes of life, but only if you learned to shed the vanity of self-consciousness and allowed the poem to speak for itself. She understood that writing is an endeavor that is born in solitude but that ultimately embraces a host of other people.[73]

Is not the monastic way similar, a diminishment of egotistical pursuit?

If Thomas Merton hadn't become friendly with people like Robert Lax at New York's Columbia University, I fear he may have become a mediocre writer eventually succumbing to alcoholism. Which makes me wonder what would've happened to the naïve, inexperienced Norris if Betty Kray hadn't taken her under her wing.

If Betty Kray taught Norris how to live, she also taught her how to die. Kray gave away her possessions, a stripping away process reminiscent of the stage of the mystical journey named Purgation.

But there are always "things" to remind Norris of her dear friend Betty: like a special bench in Central Park where they both would enjoy a "pretzel from a vendor, a piece of fruit, a container of yogurt from a deli."[74]

Norris's poetry reminds me of Anne Porter's *An Altogether Different Language*, a collection of 115 short poems gleaned from sixty years of writing verse in obscurity. When I wrote to Mrs. Porter (widow of painter Fairfield Porter), I asked her if she could offer me any information about my new discovery the poet James Schuyler's religious faith at the end of his life. She referred me to p. 241 of his *Collected Poetry* where he describes himself as a crypto-Catholic, hoping to die within the Church.

Both Porter and Norris employ a brief, austere poetic line. Porter would've produced much more verse had she not been the mother of five children, one autistic, about whom she wrote, "My Son Johnny," an exquisitely poignant lyric about maternal love.

Norris is childless, but like her mentor Betty Kray she loves children, which explains her joy in teaching them about poetry, a vocation unto itself.

Both Porter and Norris love the sky, finding beauty and repose by simply watching it. Two kindred souls. And now I'm wondering if Anne Porter (b. 1911) is still alive. When I wrote to her, she was in her nineties. (She is still alive and well.)

Norris's poetic aesthetic,

A poem, after all, renders an experience that is more than mere opinion, idea, or doctrine. And it is as experience that a poem stands or falls, inviting the reader not to debate or argue but to respond with both heart and mind.[75]

At the end of *The Virgin of Bennington*, Norris looks back upon her youthful mistakes with a forgiving eye. All the people she met, the successes and the blunders, pour into the mix that made her the woman she is. She admits that when she thought God was absent from her life, he was really present, "God was there, a silent watcher and infinitely patient companion, waiting for me to come to my senses."[76]

Norris is excited about the current pursuit of biblical exegesis. How surprised I was to read that Jesus' words "The kingdom of God is within you" is now translated in the New Revised Standard Version as "The kingdom of God is *among* you." Quite a different translation with quite a different message!

Betty Kray knew about Norris's close friendship with the Benedictines, how they provided Norris with fresh inspiration for both her writing and daily living. Before her death, Kray said to Norris, "I like the person you're becoming."

Norris embraces her comment as a bestowed blessing, a confirmation that she's heading in the right direction in her life, perhaps the road less traveled by but for her the right road.

The last page of *The Virgin of Bennington* shows a photograph of Betty Kray.

The complaint of most of the reviews about *The Virgin of Bennington* is that, as I've already mentioned, it gives too much space to Kray's life. But after a rereading, I think I know what Norris was up to: she's trying to see herself through Betty's eyes. Betty had always held aloft the standards by which Norris measured herself. Kray becomes the litmus test; and Norris remains hesitant about whether or not she passed. She writes,

But it remains an open question...as long as I keep asking whether the person I am is, in this moment, someone Betty would want to befriend, I know now that God works with us as we are, and through other people becomes incarnate to us. When I pray Psalm 25, "Do not remember the sins of my youth, but in your love remember me," it is Betty's vigilant, vigorous, and loyal love that I think of, as I give thanks to God.[77]

I think Betty Kray would be proud of the woman Norris is and is still becoming. And I look forward to more poetry from her, and perhaps another autobiographical account, one more about herself, and about how she coped with her husband's ill health and death, a momentous event for any loving and caring wife.

For the reader without the time to read all three of Norris's autobiographies, I suggest that much of her spiritual journey can be found in one poem, "A Letter to Paul Carroll, Who Said I Must Become a Catholic so That I Can Pray for Him."

It's here, in the silent monastery corridor,
I think of you and say a prayer
for those lost by the way,
for the foolish virgins,
not the wise. It's your prayer, too, Paul,
for the losers
of eternal life, the unfaithful
departed, who sit alone
in the near-dark, writing
Why—do they shut Me out of Heaven?

You and I know that now
Miss Emily Dickinson descends a staircase
in the Elysian Fields. With her is
Miss Thérèse of Lisieux,
who said to Jesus,
I am happy not enjoying the sight of that beautiful heaven
Here on earth, as long as you open it in eternity
For unbelievers. Here, Paul, where they pray
and cross themselves
and tend bees and run a print shop
and farm and come to choir
stinking of sweat. They're Catholic enough
even for you, and their prayers rise like incense
carried by the angels up to God.
Of course I believe it. Even the Methodist
in me believes in the change,
the bread and wine that turns into Benedictines
dressed like ravens
who reappear each morning
to pray and sing.
Of course I don't belong
In habits as black as unbelief, as black
as the Black Madonna,
who answers all prayers from the heart,
they take me in out of charity.

When I'm among them
I say all the "Glorias"
and "Alleluias" and "Amens,"

and often I really mean it.
I don't know what I'm saying,
Paul, and that's the point.[78]

It's rather touching that Norris identifies with the lost, the foolish virgins, the unfaithful, and the lonely sitting in the dark.

Poets who've converted to Catholicism: Thomas Merton, William Everson (Brother Antoninus), Anne Porter, Denise Levertov, Annie Dillard, and Franz Wright. Will Norris become a Catholic?

Norris's icons are Miss Emily Dickinson and Miss Thérèse of Liseux: Both are women, both poets, one a secular saint, the other a canonized saint; both had experienced the dark night of the soul.

Norris is moved by St. Thérèse's love for unbelievers, dedicated to praying them into heaven. Norris is an intellectual who likely grapples with doubt on a daily basis. In fact, I would hazard to guess that most intelligent people struggle with doubt in the midst of their faith-*full* lives. Even Christ experienced fear and doubt.

Norris prays the Glorias, the Alleluias, and the Amens. She also says she doesn't know what she's saying, and that's the point because faith is based not so much on knowledge as it is on belief in things unseen. Such a leap of faith demands courage of which St. Thérèse possessed much.

At the threshold of death, having suffered terribly from consumption, the saint of the Little Way enters upon her darkest night, losing her belief in the immortality of the soul. Only by sheer will and the grace of God is she able to hang on to a single gleam of light:

> When I sing of Heaven's happiness, of what it is to possess God for ever, I feel no joy; I simply sing of what I want to believe. Now and then, I must admit, a gleam of light shines through the dark night, to bring a moment's respite, but afterwards its memory, instead of consoling me, only makes my night darker than ever.[79]

Too often people think it's easy to believe, but Norris knows that it's difficult and sometimes a burden. But there are moments when we're as certain as Emily Dickinson is in her charmingly brief lyric,

> I never saw a Moor—
> I never saw the Sea—
> Yet know I how the Heather looks
> And what a Billow be.

> I never spoke with God
> Nor visited in Heaven—
> Yet certain am I of the spot
> As if the Charts were given—[80]

Such a wise description of faith—and hope.

As I have done with my two previous "Walking with" books, I'd like to end my walk with Kathleen Norris with a letter of appreciation.

A Letter to Kathleen Norris

～～

Dear Kathleen Norris,

You and I are baby boomers. We grew up in an America that included tremendous political, social, and religious upheavals. Like you, I was a confused child of the 1960s, searching for meaning amidst the chaos of the time. We questioned everything, from our sexual mores to our political and religious traditions, and much of it we too hastily rejected, creating a void we often thought could be filled with money, career, and sex.

You grew up with a "Monster God," and so had I. So frightening was the image of God presented to me by family and teachers that I turned to the East in search of peace and wholeness. And although I found serenity, it was not the Buddha I needed but Jesus Christ, his presence always within me; thus, I returned to the faith into which I was baptized to reexamine the religion I so cavalierly discarded.

We also share a love and appreciation of Thomas Merton. He was my constant, unwavering connection to my Church when I wandered the East. Like him, you are a religious poet, considered like him a minor poet, but you are major in the influence of your prose, again like Merton. Just recently in *In the Dark Before Dawn: New Selected Poems of Thomas Merton,* you comment on one of Merton's invaluable gifts to our time,

"What may be most valuable for the contemporary reader is the way that Merton's poems offer evidence that ecstasy, and specifically religious ecstasy, is still possible in this world, and still meaningful."[81] Yours is the perfect retort to an eminent literary critic who says that modern poets don't write about transcendence. Well, many do, including Merton and you.

You find spiritual sustenance in the Benedictine community where you hear and chant the psalms on a daily basis. Benedictine life is imbued with the Old and New Testament as well as the Rule of St. Benedict. The psalms and the Rule moved you, even to your becoming a Benedictine oblate. From flower child to oblate is a huge leap, one that has offered you not only a sacred space to pursue your deepening relationship with God but also a locus for the enriching friendships you've made with Benedictine monks.

Similarly I've found a sacred place in St. Joseph's Abbey, a Cistercian monastery here in Massachusetts. For thirty years I have attended retreats at St. Joseph's, encountering kindness and holiness among the monks who are living icons: Christ radiates from their faces.

Like the writings of the famous Cistercian Thomas Merton, your work, both prose and poetry, has resonated with American readers. You articulate for so many of us our soul hunger and thirst for a deeper spiritual life. In particular, your best-selling *The Cloister Walk* mirrors our search for spiritual sustenance. Too many of us had been too caught up in the American Dream, unquestioningly believing that the more things we possess, the happier we'll be. We've only recently realized that such thinking is the Great Lie of the last century. We may have freed our libidos, but we've naively succumbed to a more insidious repression: the denial of the spiritual impulse. And this has led to all kinds of unhappiness if not various enervating, soul-numbing neuroses.

Thank you for sharing your journey. And thank you pointing us in the right direction, to where we can still find the "peace that passeth understanding": it's as near as the closest church, or if we're fortunate in our surroundings, the nearest abbey.

God speed,

Robert Waldron

Epilogue

⁓ ⁓

Placing Kathleen Norris within the context of twentieth-century spiritual autobiographies isn't difficult. She continues the tradition of Thomas Merton's *The Seven Storey Mountain*, likely one of the most read autobiographies of our time. When it was first published, Fulton Sheen compared it to Augustine's *Confessions*, a description likely the result of Merton's veiled references to a libertine life, similar to the pre-conversion life of Augustine of Hippo. But after a close reading, most readers saw little evidence of such a life, except for Merton's mention of partying and drinking, his seemingly "worst sins," albeit typical rites of passage for most modern young people.

Merton's lack of commentary on his erotic escapades in Cambridge, England, and New York City is more than likely the result of close scrutiny of his order's censors. Only when Monica Furlong published her unauthorized biography did we learn why Merton had left England: he'd fathered a child and his guardian Tom Bennett (Merton was by then an orphan), doubtful that Merton would ever pass a background check for Civil Service, had advised him to return to America to live with his grandparents.

Merton aficionados then looked forward to the publication of Merton's unexpurgated journals, expecting to find a more detailed account of his life as a young, sexually liberated modern man. But except for his frank description of his affair with his nurse when he was in his early fifties (although he never confessed to consummating the affair), there isn't the kind of candidness about eroticism found in Norris's memoirs. But to be fair, Merton was of a different generation for whom discussion of such intimacies was considered bad taste. Norris is a child of the sexual revolution of the 1960s, free of such inhibitions.

But these two memoirists have much in common. Like Merton, Norris searched for love in all the wrong places. Like him, she lived at the center of American culture, New York City with its "nightspots, taxicabs, rooftops, railroad apartments, seedy lofts, and elegant townhouses."[82] Her New York of the 1970s was not much different from New York of the 1930s when Merton lived on Perry Street with its tenements, bars, Harlem jazz joints, screaming kids playing on the streets during sizzling summers, and gunshots heard throughout the night.

Both Merton and Norris were ambivalent about New York; they loved its frenetic energy, its multiculturalism, its people, but they also recognized that it wasn't a place to find their souls. These two artists would eventually choose rural over urban life, one drawn to a Cistercian abbey in the Kentucky hills, the other to a Benedictine abbey in the Midwest: both submitting themselves to life according to the ancient Rule of St. Benedict, overtly antithetical to the mores of contemporary life.

So enamored is Norris of Benedictine spirituality, that she, along with Esther de Waal and Joan Chittister, has become one of our leading authorities on life according to the Rule, eloquently and insightfully writing about it in her memoirs and elsewhere. And she has also elected to become a Benedictine oblate. She writes,

An oblation is an abbreviated yet powerful profession of monastic vows; you attach yourself to a particular monastery by signing a document on the altar during Mass, in which you promise to follow the Rule of St. Benedict insofar as your situation in life will allow.[83]

In youth, poets had been Norris's priests, in adulthood, the composition of poetry served as a refuge in Norris's life; poetry buttressed her sanctuary with Benedictine monks, who believe that transcendence can be found in a life dedicated to work and prayer. By chanting psalms along with the monks, a whole new world opened for Norris: in the Psalter she meets a poetry that speaks to her of the possibility of peace of soul and of an intimate relationship with God.

As poets, Norris and Merton appreciate the psalms as part of the canon of the world's greatest poems, but more importantly they also find spiritual sustenance in them. Norris would likely agree that Merton's comment also applies to lay people,

> For the monk who really enters into the full meaning of his vocation, the Psalms are the nourishment of his interior life, and form the material of his meditations and of his personal prayer, so that at last he comes to live them and experience them as if they were his own songs, his own prayers.[84]

Placing Norris within the context of modern poetry is much more problematic. She's not listed in our major anthologies (neither is Thomas Merton). One wonders why. Perhaps Norris and Merton are considered too minor, perhaps too religious. When

David Shapiro submitted Anne Porter's verse to an editor, he described her as perhaps the greatest living Catholic or religious poet. The editor's response was "Why then, forget it."[85]

Norris is listed, however, in David Impastato's ground-breaking *Upholding Mystery: An Anthology of Contemporary Christian Poetry* (Oxford University Press) along with such distinguished poets as Daniel Berrigan, Wendell Berry, Annie Dillard, Geoffrey Hill, Andrew Hudgins, Denise Levertov, Richard Wilbur, and others.

The impetus behind Impastato's collection is a remark by literary critic Helen Vendler, "There is no significant poet whose work does not mirror, both formally and in its preoccupations, the absence of the transcendent—in other words no poet today writes religious poetry."[86] As was Impastato, I'm astonished by her comment (how ironic that one of her books of essays is titled *Soul Says*) because the poets I currently read have all written verse undoubtedly mirroring an abiding belief in transcendence: Anne Porter, Marie Ponsot, Mary Oliver, Paul Mariani, Mary Karr, Mark Jarman, Vassar Miller, John Berryman, Franz Wright (recent winner of the Pulitzer Prize and a convert to Catholicism), and particularly Jane Kenyon; after her death, Kenyon has emerged as one of our most important religious poets.

A cursory look at Norris's *Journey: New and Selected Poems, 1969–1999* illustrates that by the time Norris enters the 1990s, more and more of her poems address overtly Christian themes: "A Poem about Faith," "Little Girls in Church," "The Monastery Orchard in Early Spring," "Epiphany," "Mysteries of the Incarnation," "Luke 14: A Commentary," "Naming the Living God," "The Presbyterian Women Serve Coffee at the Home." Even the three poems I've used in my diary are spiritual exercises: "Perennials" is a poem about faith, "Eve of St. Agnes in the High School Gym" is about love, and "A Letter to Paul Carroll, Who Said I Must Become a Catholic so That I Can Pray for Him" is about forgiveness.

Throughout her life, poetry offered strength to Norris, one of its primary purposes according to her mentor Betty Kray. Writing poetry is also holy ground for Norris. Too often we equate geography with holy ground, as Norris does for the plains in her *Dakota: A Spiritual Geography*. Holy ground can, indeed, be midwestern plains, a monastic cloister, a chapel, a cathedral, or even one's garden. There's much to be said for a connection with the earth, dirtying our hands by gardening, a pastime Norris learned after inheriting her grandmother's garden. But the pure blank white space of a page is also a *locus Dei*, where Norris composes her own psalms, poems reflecting her search for peace and divine intimacy.

To create a word-icon of a poem, the poet must embark upon the inner journey and approach the *kapporeth*, the mercy-seat of the soul. Rowan Williams writes,

> In old Jerusalem, the heart of the city was the Temple, and the heart of the Temple was the throne, the *kapporeth*, or mercy-seat—the empty space above the Ark of the Covenant, between the two golden cherubim....To go and see God in Jerusalem is to look at the curtained holy place and know that behind it is the empty space from which mercy and promise come forth, the "help from the sanctuary" and the "answer from heaven" referred to in the psalms.[87]

She has gazed upon the *kapporeth* and sometimes she's been terrified, but more often than not she's been granted mercy to capture her soul's whispers of intuitions, hints, guesses, and appreciations later to be transformed into beautiful verse; she finds the All in Nothing—*todo y nada* of St. John of the Cross—that leads to Christ. Merton says, "Christ is the inspiration of Christian poetry, and Christ is the center of the contemplative life."[88] Therefore, a poet like Norris is just as Christ-like when she's composing poetry as when she's chanting the psalms with her Benedictine community or in the privacy of her home.

Over the years, Norris has created her Psalter, composed from her contemplative experience. Her every poem, composed by and through contemplative attention, is a prayer. And when we the reader offer her poetry our complete attention, we "pray" her poems, joining our voice with hers, as well as with all those members of the Mystical Body of Christ praying throughout this world and the next.

John Ashbery says, "poetry is not a stationery object but a kinetic act, in which something is transferred from somebody to somebody else."[89] What, we may well ask, is transferred by Norris to her reader? Surely it's her faith and hope in and her love of God. Thus she offers spiritual sustenance to her readers, the greatest gift any artist can offer.

Without any doubt on my part, Kathleen Norris is one of our great spiritual memoirists, as well as a fine poet: she's a poet who has something vital to share, and she altruistically reaches out to touch her readers with prose and poems announcing God's presence here and now. All we have to do is open our eyes and pay attention.

Endnotes

❧ ❧

1. Kathleen Norris, *The Cloister Walk* (New York: Riverhead Books, 1996), p. 91.

2. Ibid., p. 98.

3. Ibid., p. 99.

4. Ibid., p. 91.

5. Ibid., p. 63.

6. Ibid., p. 382.

7. Ibid., p. 65.

8. Matthew Arnold, *Poems* (London: MacMillan and Co., 1895), p. 214.

9. Kathleen Norris, *Journey: New and Selected Poems, 1969–1999* (Pittsburgh: University of Pittsburgh Press, 2001), p. 45.

10. Kathleen Norris, *Dakota: A Spiritual Geography* (Boston: Houghton Mifflin, 1993), p. 15.

11. *Little Girls in Church* (Pittsburgh: University of Pittsburgh Press, 1995), p. 19.

12. *Dakota*, p. 44.

13. Ibid., p. 9.

14. *Boston Globe*, April 22, 2002.

15. Ibid.

16. Esther de Waal, *A Life-Giving Way: A Commentary on the Rule of St. Benedict* (Collegeville, MN: The Liturgical Press, 1995).

17. *Cloister Walk*, p. 35.

18. Ibid., p. 48.

19. *Dakota*, p. 89.

20. Ibid., p. 92.

21. Ibid., p. 97.

22. Ibid.

23. Ibid., p. 94.

24. Ibid., p. 96.

25. Ibid., p. 183.

26. Samuel Taylor Coleridge, *Selected Poems* (New York: St. Martin's Press, 1994), p, 20.

27. *Dakota*, p. 185.

28. Ibid., p. 203.

29. *Cloister Walk*, p. 96.

30. Ibid., p. 97.

31. Ibid., p. 107.

32. Ibid., p. 201.

33. *Dakota*, p. 23.

34. Ibid., p. 21.

35. Ibid., p. 18.

36. Ibid., p. 189.

37. William Shakespeare, *Hamlet*, Act 3, Scene 1.

38. Ibid.

39. *Dakota*, p. 43.

40. *Hamlet*, Act 3, Scene 3.

41. Ibid.

42. *Dakota*, p. 60.

43. *Life-Giving Way*, p. xi.

44. Robert Waldron, *Catholic Digest*, April 1996.

45. Linda Pastan, *Carnival Evening: New and Selected Poems, 1968–1998* (New York: W. W. Norton, 1998), p. 38.

46. Kathleen Norris, *Amazing Grace: A Vocabulary of Faith* (New York: Riverhead Books, 1998), p. 317.

47. *Carnival*, p. 38.

48. James Wright, *Collected Poems* (Middletown, CT: Wesleyan University Press, 1971), p. 114.

49. *Journey*, p. 63.

50. *Amazing Grace*, p. 165.

51. *Journey*, p. 55.

52. *Cloister Walk*, Norris quoting William Stafford, *A Message from Oregon*, p. 143.

53. Kathleen Norris, *The Virgin of Bennington* (New York: Riverhead Books, 2001), p. 56.

54. Ibid., p. 57.

55. Joan D. Chittister, *The Rule of Benedict: Insights for the Ages* (New York: Crossroad, 1992), p. 51.

56. Ibid.

57. Philip Toynbee, *Part of a Journey: An Autobiographical Journal, 1977–1979* (London: Collins, 1981), p. 42.

58. *Amazing Grace*, p. 125.

59. Letter to author from Kathleen Raine.

60. *Virgin*, p. 3.

61. From unpublished novel, *The Exquisite Risk*.

62. Willa Cather, *My Antonia* (Boston: Houghton Mifflin, 1995), p. 7.

63. *Amazing Grace*, p. 282.

64. *Virgin*, p. 47.

65. Ibid., p. 50.

66. Ibid., p. 123.

67. Ibid., p. 93.

68. Personal letter from Kathleen Raine.

69. Peggy Rosenthal, *Praying through Poetry: Hope for Violent Times* (Cincinnati: St. Anthony Messenger Press, 2003). p. v.

70. *Virgin*, p. 237.

71. *Journey*, p. 117.

72. Ibid., p. 128.

73. *Virgin*, p. 241.

74. Ibid., p. 243.

75. Ibid., p. 248.

76. Ibid.

77. Ibid., p. 250.

78. *Journey*, p. 78.

79. Ida Freiderike Görres, *The Hidden Face* (San Francisco: Ignatius Press, 2003), p. 354.

80. Emily Dickinson, *The Complete Poems of Emily Dickinson*, ed. Thomas H. Johnson (Boston: Little, Brown and Company, 1955), p. 480.

81. Thomas Merton, *In the Dark Before Dawn: New Selected Poems of Thomas Merton*, Preface, Kathleen Norris; ed. Lynn R. Szabo (New York: A New Directions Book, 2005), p. xvii.

82. Quoted from the book cover of *The Virgin of Bennington*.

83. *Cloister Walk*, p. xi.

84. Thomas Merton, *Bread in the Wilderness* (New York: A New Directions Book, 1953), p. 3.

85. Anne Porter, *Living Things: Collected Poems* (Hanover, NH: Zoland Books, 2006), p. xi.

86. Quoted from the book cover of David Impastato's, *Upholding Mystery: An Anthology of Contemporary Christian Poetry*.

87. Rowan Williams, *A Ray of Darkness: Sermons and Reflections* (Cambridge: Cowley Publications. 1995), p. 85.

88. Thomas Merton, *The Literary Essays of Thomas Merton* (New York: A New Directions Book, 1981), p. 341.

89. John Ashbery, *Selected Prose* (Ann Arbor: University of Michigan Press, 2004), p. 211.

Bibliography

Arnold, Matthew. *Poems*. London: Macmillan and Co., 1895.

Ashbery, John. *Selected Prose*. Ann Arbor: University of Michigan Press, 2004.

Augustine, Saint. *The Confessions of St. Augustine*. Translated by Maria Baulding. New York: New City Press, 2002.

Cather, Willa. *My Antonia*. Foreword by Kathleen Norris. Boston: Houghton Mifflin, 1995.

Chittister, Joan D. *The Rule of Benedict: Insights for the Ages*. New York: Crossroad, 1992.

Coleridge, Samuel Taylor. *Selected Poems*. New York: St. Martin's Press, 1994.

Dickinson, Emily. *The Complete Poems of Emily Dickinson*. Edited by Thomas H. Johnson. Boston: Little, Brown and Company, 1955.

Fry, Timothy, editor. *The Rule of St. Benedict*. Collegeville: The Liturgical Press, 1981.

Görres, Ida Friederike. *The Hidden Face: A Study of St. Thérèse of Lisieux*. San Francisco: Ignatius Press, 2003.

Impastato, David. *Upholding Mystery: An Anthology of Contemporary Christian Poetry*. New York: Oxford University Press, 1997.

Merton, Thomas. *Bread in the Wilderness*. New York: A New Directions Book, 1953.

——————. *In the Dark Before Dawn: New Selected Poems of Thomas Merton*. Preface by Kathleen Norris; edited by Lynn R. Szabo. New York: A New Directions Book, 2005.

——————. *The Literary Essays of Thomas Merton*. New York: A New Directions Book, 1981.

——————. *The Seven Storey Mountain*. New York: Harcourt, Brace and Company, 1948.

Norris, Kathleen. *Amazing Grace: A Vocabulary of Faith*. New York: Riverhead Books, 1998.

——————. *The Cloister Walk*. New York: Riverhead Books, 1996.

——————. *Dakota: A Spiritual Geography*. Boston: Houghton Mifflin, 1993.

——————. *Journey: New and Selected Poems, 1969–1999*. Pittsburgh: University of Pittsburgh Press, 2001.

——————. *Little Girls in Church*. Pittsburgh: University of Pittsburgh Press, 1995.

——————. *The Virgin of Bennington*. New York: Riverhead Books, 2001.

Pastan, Linda. *Carnival Evening: New and Selected Poems, 1968–1998*. New York: W. W. Norton, 1998.

Porter, Anne. *Living Things: Collected Poems*. Hanover, NH: Zoland Books, 2006.

Rosenthal, Peggy. *Praying through Poetry: Hope for Violent Times*. Cincinnati: St. Anthony Messenger Press, 2003.

Shakespeare, William. *Hamlet*. New York: The New Folger Library Shakespeare, 1992.

Toynbee, Philip. *Part of a Journey: An Autobiographical Journal, 1977–1979*. London: Collins, 1981.

de Waal, Esther. *A Life-Giving Way: A Commentary on the Rule of St. Benedict*. Collegeville, MN: The Liturgical Press, 1995.

Williams, Rowan. *A Ray of Darkness: Sermons and Reflections*. Cambridge: Cowley Publications, 1995.

Wright, James. *Collected Poems*. Middletown, CT: Wesleyan University Press, 1971.